'This book provides a very useful extensio  h to managing children and teenagers with ASD oice and self-advocacy in those for whom cognitiv ered such skills a challenge.'
— *Trevor Sim, Principal Educational psychologist, London Borough of Havering*

'Linda's second book builds upon the successful 5P approach for behaviour management and tackles the tricky area of developing flexibility which impacts individuals with autism. The book is accessible, illuminates the issues and develops understanding of this critical area and provides a framework for practitioners and parents to baseline, plan intervention and track progress. This is an exciting and essential tool for those working to improve the lives of people with autism.'
— *Adrienne Wright, Head Teacher, Kestrel House School London*

'A fresh, new insight into autism practice and a successful attempt to redefine the child-centred specialist approach through a step-by-step structured assessment of flexibility skills. This book will constitute an essential guide for professionals and entire organisations working with children with poor flexibility skills and which aim at creating the foundation for development of independence and successful learning.'
— *Andrea Centonze, Senior Assistant Psychologist, Kestrel House School*

'An excellent book which will be of enormous benefit for those interested in understanding the impact of flexibility in children on children's learning, social behaviour and independence. Linda Miller builds on previous research and writes in a language which is accessible to both lay and professional people. As such, it is the first book on flexibility in its own right which combines theory, assessment tools and practical strategies. A must for parents/carers, teachers, professionals, schools and other organisations!'
— *Esther Fenty, educational psychologist*

by the same author

**Practical Behaviour Management Solutions for
Children and Teens with Autism
The 5P Approach**
Linda Miller
ISBN 978 1 84905 038 8
eISBN 978 0 85700 184 9

of related interest

**Helping Students Take Control of Everyday Executive Functions
The Attention Fix**
Paula Moraine
ISBN 978 1 84905 884 1
eISBN 978 1 85700 576 2

**Teaching Theory of Mind
A Curriculum for Children with High Functioning Autism,
Asperger's Syndrome, and Related Social Challenges**
Kirstina Ordetx
Foreword by Susan J. Moreno
ISBN 978 1 84905 897 1

**A Practical Guide for Teachers of Students with an Autism
Spectrum Disorder in Secondary Education**
Debra Costley, Elaine Keane, Trevor Clark and Kathleen Lane
ISBN 978 1 84905 310 5
eISBN 978 0 85700 646 2

**Helping Children with Autism Spectrum Conditions
through Everyday Transitions
Small Changes – Big Challenges**
John Smith, Jane Donlan and Bob Smith
ISBN 978 1 84905 275 7
eISBN 978 0 85700 572 4

DEVELOPING FLEXIBILITY SKILLS IN CHILDREN AND TEENS WITH AUTISM

The 5P Approach to Thinking, Learning and Behaviour

Linda Miller

Jessica Kingsley *Publishers*
London and Philadelphia

First published in 2013
by Jessica Kingsley Publishers
116 Pentonville Road
London N1 9JB, UK
and
400 Market Street, Suite 400
Philadelphia, PA 19106, USA

www.jkp.com

Library of Congress Cataloging in Publication Data
Miller, Linda (Linda Janice)
  Developing flexibility skills in children and teens with autism : using the 5P approach / Linda Miller.
    pages cm
  Includes bibliographical references and index.
  ISBN 978-1-84905-362-4 (alk. paper)
  1. Autism in children. 2. Autism in adolescence. 3. Motor ability in children. I. Title.
  RJ506.A9M5848 2013
  618.92'85882--dc23
                          2012046245

British Library Cataloguing in Publication Data
A CIP catalogue record for this book is available from the British Library

ISBN 978 1 84905 362 4
eISBN 978 0 85700 711 7

Printed and bound in Great Britain

This book could not have been written without the help of all those 5P practitioners who have tried and tested these ideas and materials and who have been a continuing source of help and encouragement over a number of years.

I would particularly like to thank my husband Ian for all his support and words of wisdom and Louise for providing inspiration, practical ideas and art work.

CONTENTS

LIST OF TABLES

LIST OF FIGURES

INTRODUCTION

About this Book

Those who work with or care for individuals on the autistic spectrum will have first-hand experience of a common behaviour pattern – a difficulty in showing flexibility in how they think and what they do. In fact, it is one of the areas of the triad of impairments which characterise the condition. Typified by a lack of adaptability, rigid behaviour, narrow interests, obsessions and poor problem-solving skills, impaired flexibility is often the cause of behaviour difficulty and presents a considerable barrier to learning.

But while there is no doubt that poor flexibility has a huge impact on behaviour, learning, social development and independence, it is often the area least talked about in terms of intervention. This book sets out to shine some light on this important area, and provide a comprehensive solution with which to approach it. First, it provides a comprehensive framework for teachers, parents and professionals to support children and young people with autism and related disorders and to help them develop flexibility skills and increased independence. Second, it provides a means of reducing behaviour issues which arise from poor flexibility.

Flexibility or flexible thinking is about the way we process information and how this in turn affects learning and behaviour. When we examine the origins of flexibility, the ability to regulate and control our thought processes, known as executive function, is a key factor. Difficulties with executive function are shared by many individuals with or without a diagnosis of autism, all of whom may have difficulties such as those described above. In particular, those who have a diagnosis of other neurodevelopmental disorders such as Attention Deficit Hyperactivity Disorder (ADHD), Dyspraxia and so forth exhibit problems with executive function and flexible thinking. As such, the 5P Approach to Flexibility described within this book is equally applicable to any individual who displays the characteristic difficulties associated with poor flexibility and poor executive function regardless of diagnosis.

This book takes a detailed look at flexibility and its relationship to independence, learning, social development and behaviour. Using the principles and philosophy of the 5P Approach, it provides a framework for flexibility assessment and intervention planning at the individual level and also at the organisational level.

The 5P Approach to behaviour intervention was introduced in the book *Practical Behaviour Management Solutions for Children and Teens with Autism* (Miller 2009). The 5P Approach uses the distinctive GREEN-AMBER-RED traffic light colours to distinguish levels of behaviour and places the emphasis on using different strategies at the different levels. It provides a complete framework for behaviour intervention which has its roots in prevention and good practice (GREEN), with an emphasis on promoting and encouraging the development of skills and independence, through using the 5Ps – Profiling, Prioritising, Problem analysis, Problem solving and Planning. Over the past three years the 5P Approach has grown and developed. The philosophy and principles represented within the unique traffic light colour system are now widely used by both professionals and parents.

The 5P Approach to Flexibility, introduced in this book, builds upon this and places a focus specifically on flexibility. As with the 5P Approach to behaviour intervention, the 5P Approach to Flexibility emphasises the importance of developing skills and creating foundations (a GREEN Zone) which provide a safe and supportive environment, promote the development of independence and reduce behaviour issues which arise from poor flexibility.

The strategies and framework set out in this book are designed specifically to take account of what we know about flexibility and to support the individual to overcome the barriers to learning that poor flexibility creates.

What this book does

This book outlines a complete flexibility *framework*. Starting with understanding the nature of flexibility and looking at the implications of poor flexibility on learning, social development and independence, the 5P Approach to Flexibility sets out a structured intervention pathway from assessment to intervention planning.

It provides a complete 'toolkit' for both professionals and carers that includes practical activities and ideas and a range of templates and visual representations which support the overall approach. The aim is to provide the reader with everything they need to work with children and young people with flexibility difficulty and to support them to make progress and develop independence.

Using the 5P principle that knowing the individual well (the first 'P') is the first step in the intervention process, the book introduces the 5P Approach Flexibility Assessment. This comprehensive checklist can be used to identify areas of strength and those for development. The book introduces the concept of the Flexibility Continuum which provides a pathway for flexibility development.

Using the 5P traffic lights, the 5P Approach Flexibility Strands represent a four strand framework for intervention planning. The four strands: creating a GREEN

Zone or foundations, developing flexibility skills, providing opportunity to use flexibility skills and supporting the development of coping or self-management strategies, work together to create a supportive environment which encourages the development of skill and maximises opportunities for the individual to make progress. Small step progress can be measured through regular assessment and plotted on the Individual Flexibility Continuum.

This book also takes a look at the links between flexibility and enabling participation or giving individuals a 'voice'. Developing flexibility is identified as being crucial to the development of those skills an individual needs to participate in decision making and to express their views. Closely linked to flexibility, the development of self-knowledge and self-expression are also key to successful participation. This book introduces two further assessment tools: the 5P Approach Assessment of Self-knowledge and the 5P Approach Expressing Views Assessment which complement the 5P Approach Flexibility Assessment and are designed in the same general format. Together these three assessment tools form a comprehensive pack which specifically targets this area.

What makes it different?

Several books and materials describe the implications of poor flexibility in individuals with autism and related disorders such as the *Autistic Spectrum Disorders: Good Practise Guidance* (DfES and DoH 2002) and the National Strategies *Inclusion Development Programme Primary and Secondary: Supporting Pupils on the Autism Spectrum* (DCSF 2009) but few look at the area as whole and even fewer look at this as a particular area in its own right. Flexibility is often linked with behaviour issues and anxiety and is frequently an underlying factor when difficulties with learning arise but nonetheless there are very few materials which support flexibility assessment and planning.

This book sets out to redress this balance by providing a complete framework which looks at the area as a *whole*. The focus on addressing the four Flexibility Strands provides a unique framework for intervention planning at the individual and organisational level. Together with the 5P Approach to behaviour intervention, the 5P Approach to Flexibility provides a comprehensive range of ideas, materials and resources aimed at preventing issues form arising and developing a supportive environment in which the individual can move forward and make progress.

The 5P Approach places an emphasis on consistency of approach and on the importance of team work. The materials within this book are designed to encourage those working with the individual (and the individuals themselves) to develop common understanding, common language and common goals. The 5P framework adopts a model of learning from experience, building on new knowledge and successful strategies and adding these to an ever-expanding GREEN Zone.

The 5P Approach to Flexibility and all the materials introduced within this book have been used time and time again within training sessions and within schools, homes and organisations by a range of professionals and carers. As with the 5P Approach to behaviour intervention, materials, ideas and resources have been modified and expanded over time taking account of the people who use them within their everyday work. The 5P Approach to Flexibility has been used widely to assess and plan programmes with a range of individuals of all ages and abilities.

As you will see from the early chapters of this book, children and young people with flexibility difficulties often struggle to develop skills or make progress at a rate similar to their flexible peers. For those who get it right, flexibility is one area where schools and organisations can make a real difference and can support individuals to make progress in a short space of time. However, flexibility skills are rarely assessed and monitored and do not appear as a separate area in any curriculum-based assessment scheme. Individuals may make good progress (and move along the Flexibility Continuum) but there is no way of demonstrating or monitoring this. The 5P Approach Flexibility Assessment (and the accompanying 5P Assessment of Self-knowledge and 5P Expressing Views Assessment) provides a means of assessing, monitoring and tracking progress across time in areas so often missed within other formal assessment systems. The format is such that even if the individual does not make sufficient progress to move up a level, small step progress can be monitored through changes in percentage or raw scores.

How this book is set out

This book begins with an overview of what you need to know about flexibility, its origins and the implications of poor flexibility on learning, social development, behaviour and independence.

This is followed by an overview of the 5P Approach to Flexibility as set out within this book. The book then looks in detail at the assessment of flexibility skills using the 5P Approach Flexibility Assessment, how this can be used and how this links to intervention planning.

This also includes general ideas and resources and looks specifically at areas which pose a particular problem for those with flexibility issues, such as transitions, adaptability and problem solving.

The book goes on to look at the link between flexibility and participation or pupil voice, examining what is meant by this and what the implications are for those who may have difficulties with flexibility. This chapter identifies the key skills an individual requires to participate in decision making and express their views and introduces two further assessment tools, the 5P Approach Assessment of Self-knowledge and the 5P Approach Expressing Views Assessment which provide additional resources for intervention planning within this important area.

Chapter 7 pulls together all the information within the book and looks at how this can be used to form the basis of a flexibility policy and a flexibility curriculum. Again, there are additional ideas and resources to support this concept.

In the final chapter there are some additional case studies looking at how the 5P Approach to Flexibility and its materials can be used at the organisational and at the individual level.

How to use the book

As you can see from this introduction, this book contains a wealth of information and resources including the introduction of three assessment tools. The first thing to do is to read through to get an overview of the whole framework and process and an understanding of all the elements involved. You can do this either as an individual carer or teacher or as part of a group.

The next step is to make a start and use the guidance to begin intervention planning by using the 5P Approach Flexibility Assessment and its supporting materials.

Once familiar with this section, next steps can be to take a closer look at participation and pupil voice and finally how to use the 5P Approach to Flexibility as a basis for creation of a flexibility policy and curriculum.

For those already familiar with the 5P Approach to behaviour intervention, the links will be obvious. The 5P Approach to Flexibility will complement and extend your knowledge and resources and expand your GREEN Zone!

References

Department for Children, Schools and Families (DCSF) (2009) *Inclusion Development Programme Primary and Secondary: Supporting Pupils on the Autism Spectrum.* National Strategies. Crown Copyright. London: DCSF.

Department for Education and Skills (DfES) and Department of Health (DoH) (2002) *Autistic Spectrum Disorders: Good Practise Guidance.* Crown Copyright. London: DfES.

Miller, L. (2009) *Practical Behaviour Management Solutions for Children and Teens with Autism – The 5P Approach.* London and Philadelphia: Jessica Kingsley Publishers.

Chapter 1

WHAT IS FLEXIBILITY AND WHY IS IT IMPORTANT?

Anyone familiar with the diagnosis of autism will know that flexibility or flexibility of thought, previously known as 'imagination', is one of the areas of the triad of impairments which characterises the condition.

Originally identified by Lorna Wing and Judith Gould in 1979, the triad of impairments is still used as a basis of diagnosis of the disorder and is commonly accepted to represent the core presenting features of autism and Asperger's Syndrome. All individuals diagnosed with an autistic spectrum disorder share these three common features, although within each individual they may present in very different ways and to differing degrees. The three areas of the triad of impairments are social communication, social interaction and flexibility of thought (imagination).

Although there is speculation that one day a diagnosis of autism may be made using biological or physical features, assessing the triad of impairments in an individual still forms the basis of the diagnostic process.

The *Diagnostic and Statistical Manual of Mental Disorders: DSM IV-TR*, developed by the American Psychiatric Association (1994), and the *International Classification of Diseases 10th Edition (ICD-10)* (World Health Organization 1992) currently provide the most commonly used criteria for the diagnosis of autism or autistic disorder and Asperger's Syndrome. These both contain descriptions of unusual, stereotyped, or repetitive patterns of behaviour and narrow or restricted interests. Autism-specific clinical guidelines produced by National Institute for Health and Clinical Excellence (NICE) in 2011 also contain similar descriptions (Tables 1–3, pp.43–50).

Although not identified in name as flexibility of thought as it is in the triad of impairments, this DSM IV-TR description is consistent with the description of imagination or flexibility of thought used by Wing and Gould in their early work.

At the time of writing, the American Psychiatric Association is proposing to publish the fifth edition of the Diagnostic and Statistical Manual of Mental Disorders (DSM-V) in May 2013. This proposes a new category, Autistic Spectrum Disorder (used widely as an overall term but currently not considered to be a diagnostic term) encompassing both autism and Asperger's Syndrome. This proposed new category however contains a similar description which again appears to characterise difficulties commonly described as flexibility of thought.

To put it more generally then, a lack of flexibility in autism is commonly thought of as:

1. *Rigidity in thinking and behaviour.*

   Characterised by rigid, repetitive behaviour, difficulties with change and transition and coping with anything 'new'. For example, always using the same blue cup in school or only eating crisps with the same colour packet, always having to follow the same timetable every day, needing to see things through to the end regardless, not understanding that we may need to adapt or change our behaviour for different circumstances and so on.

2. *Ritualistic behaviour.*

   Closely linked to rigid behaviour as above, this is characterised by an individual sticking rigidly to certain routines and rituals such as always getting ready for school and packing their bag in precisely the same order, packing toys or possessions in the same way and in the same place, always walking to the shops in the same way, and visiting shops in the same order and so forth.

3. *Difficulties with selectivity or narrow focus.*

   This relates to difficulties with central coherence (see below) and difficulties with not seeing the whole picture or taking account of context to aid understanding – having such a narrow focus on one aspect of a story that you miss the plot. The term selectivity relates to someone being over 'fussy' or choosy or very selective. For example someone might be very selective about the range and type of food they eat, only wearing certain clothes. This area is also associated with paying great attention to detail which, although at times may become a problem, is also seen to be a great strength.

4. *Narrow interests and obsessions.*

   Very closely linked to selectivity above, this is characterised by sticking to a very small range of likes and interests. For example an individual may have interests in a small range of activities such as trains, engines, Star Wars, Lego and not see the need for or purpose of widening this range. At times these interests can become or be seen to become obsessive to the point that they cause behaviour issues or get in the way of learning or access to social opportunities.

The reason that a lack of flexibility is often thought of simply in these terms is likely to be because these are the areas that are associated with behaviour difficulty and with high anxiety. It is easy to see from the examples above how any of these could lead to anxiety and then to behaviour problems. It is also easy to see how, when put into the right context, some of these aspects such as attention to detail and narrow focus can become areas of strength and skills which should be used and nurtured. Taking this learning or thinking style into account is important when we look at how to use this to support individuals with autism to achieve their potential and to develop the flexibility skills they need to break down any barriers to learning. This will be addressed later in the book.

Difficulty with flexibility also affects other aspects of learning and social behaviour. This includes areas such as:

1. *Poor generalisation of skills, behaviours and knowledge.*

   If, as above, you have an approach to learning which is rigid in nature, a tendency to have a narrow focus and difficulty in making connections or seeing the wider picture, this creates a tendency to see things in isolation. If you learn a skill in one setting, without flexible thinking there is no guarantee that you will be able to (or see the need to) use that skill in another different setting, hence problems with generalisation of skills and knowledge. This of course affects the functional use or practical application of skills learned and is related to problem solving (see below).

2. *Difficulties with predicting and anticipating.*

   If you are not able to make connections, do not see the whole picture and are not able to flexibly apply the knowledge you have gained in one setting to another, this makes it difficult to predict or to anticipate what might happen next or what might happen when you meet a similar circumstance.

3. *Poor decision making and problem solving.*

   In order to make a decision there is first a need to make choices. Making choices is part of the problem-solving process. This involves being able to see the whole picture, to bring together bits of knowledge you have about the choices to be made and make judgements about them. It also involves being able to think creatively, to think of the possible options and consequences of your choice and use both these bits of information to inform your choice. This is sometimes known as convergent and divergent thinking and requires flexibility of thought. Problem solving is a complex process and also requires this type of flexible thinking. Problem solving involves the ability to identify a problem, to work out why there is a problem and what to do about it, to work out a plan of action and to evaluate how things are going.

When we look at the difficulties that result from poor flexibility what we see is behaviours that relate to or are a result of a particular way of processing information. Flexible thinking or flexibility requires the ability to use and manipulate the information and knowledge you have, to see connections between similar things and experiences, to make connections with past and previous experiences, to use what you know to be creative and imaginative, to plan, organise and sequence your responses and actions and then think back and make more connections and comparisons in order to review how things are going and adapt your approach accordingly (i.e. to learn from experience). The more difficulties an individual has with these things, the more rigid and inflexible their thinking and, in turn, the more rigid and inflexible their behaviour and learning.

If we look back at some of the examples of the behaviours listed under poor flexibility above, we can see how these inflexible behaviours might develop.

Rigidity – only using a blue cup in school

Understanding that you can use a variety of cups, glasses, mugs and so on to drink from requires the ability to make connections and see similarities in things that may look different (semantic links). It also requires the ability to make a link with using a different colour cup at home (i.e. generalising your knowledge from one place to another). However if you learn from habit that you drink from a blue cup in school and do not easily make the connections or understand 'cupness', then being given a red plastic mug to drink from one day in school doesn't seem to make sense (This isn't a cup! This isn't what I do!) and can very quickly lead to confusion, high anxiety, anger and behaviour issues.

Ritualistic behaviour – always walking to the shops in the same way and going to the same shops

People who are able to think flexibly, to make connections between events, to think back on previous experiences and problem solve are able to understand that even though there may be a preferred route to the shops, if you divert and go down a different road, have to stop because of traffic lights and so on, you will still get to the shops. If one shop is closed, flexible thinkers may be disappointed but will be able to think creatively and find another shop that sells the same thing. However to inflexible thinkers who do not have these skills this could spell disaster, leading to confusion, anxiety, anger and behaviour issues.

From these two examples above, it is easy to see how those of us with well-developed flexibility skills rely all the time on our ability to think flexibly without realising that this skill is being used. It is also easy to see how what can sometimes be seen as 'difficult' or challenging behaviour actually arises from confusion and anxiety rather than from any intention to cause a problem. Understanding and supporting the individual with poor flexibility and the teaching of flexibility skills is therefore a key to preventing behaviour difficulties from arising, ensuring the well-being of the individual concerned and to developing their independence. The 5P Approach to Flexibility sets out to address some of these issues.

In summary, poor flexibility cannot simply be described by a short list of rigid and stereotyped behaviours. Flexibility of thought or flexible thinking is a key element in many areas of skill development and is crucial to the development of independence in thinking, learning and behaviour. Flexible thinking skills are required in many aspects of play and social skill development, in thinking and understanding concepts and in being adaptable. Table 1.1 sets out a comparison between inflexible and flexible thinkers in some of these key skills.

Are problems with flexibility exclusive to autism?

The answer is no, problems with flexibility are not exclusive to autism. Although flexibility of thought is identified as one of the triad of impairments and one of the defining elements of an autism diagnosis, this is one of *three* interrelating areas required for diagnosis of autism.

Flexibility or flexible thinking is about the way we process information and how this in turn affects learning and behaviour. When we examine the origins of flexibility, the ability to regulate and control our thought processes, known as executive function, is a key factor. Difficulties with executive function are shared by many individuals with or without a diagnosis of autism, all of whom may have difficulties such as those described above. In particular, those who have a diagnosis of other neurodevelopmental disorders such as Attention Deficit Hyperactivity Disorder (ADHD), Dyspraxia, etc. exhibit problems with executive function and flexible thinking. The 5P Approach to Flexibility is equally applicable to any individual who displays the characteristic difficulties associated with poor flexibility and poor executive function regardless of diagnosis.

Table 1.1 Inflexible vs Flexible Thinkers

	Inflexible thinkers ⟶ Flexible thinkers	
Play and Social Development	Poorly developed imaginative play Repetitive/stereotyped play routines	A well-developed imaginative play – creative play using imagination, joining with others in imaginative games
	Difficulty in viewing the world from another person's perspective (Theory of Mind)	An ability to understand and accept another's point of view
	Self-interested/egocentric	An ability to share another's interests
Thinking and Conceptual Understanding	Literal interpretation of language	An understanding of implied meaning (abstract concepts, homonyms, similes, etc.)
	Difficulty in 'reading' situations	An ability to see things in context – to have an overview and take social cues
	Difficulty with inference and deduction	An ability to interpret information and understand abstract concepts
	Narrow focus/interests: • Extreme attention to detail • Restricted interests • Sensory sensitivity/sensory seeking	Having a broad focus: • Having many and varied interests • An ability to grasp bigger picture • Well-developed sensory processing
Adaptability	Rigidity in behaviour: • Insistence on/preference for routines • Demonstrating ritualistic behaviour • Difficulties with acceptance of change and transition • Poor social problem solving and planning • Difficulty in making choices • Poor 'common sense'	Flexible and adaptable behaviour: • An ability to cope with and accept change and transition • Good social problem solving and planning skills • Able to make choices • An ability to deal with everyday situations (using previous experience/knowledge)
	Rigidity in learning: • Poor generalisation • Difficulty in making choices • Poor problem solving • Poor organisation and planning skills	Flexibility in learning (accepting and coping successfully with differing approaches to learning): • Ability to transfer learned skills to new situations • Able to make choices • Good problem-solving skills • Good planning and organisation skills

Where does flexibility come from?

Over the years there has been a great deal of research looking at what might be considered to be underlying causes of those behaviours which distinguish individuals with an autism diagnosis – those behaviours which make up the triad of impairments. Three of the most prominent and long standing theories which identify difficulties or differences in the way that individuals with autism process information are Theory of Mind, Central Coherence and Executive Function. Although there appears to be some overlap and relationship between these cognitive deficit theories, they remain relatively independent of one another (Baron-Cohen and Swettenham 1997). Together they account in most part for the characteristic differences in thinking and processing of information (known as the autistic cognitive style) which in turn lead to the behaviours which manifest as those within the triad of impairments.

Two of these theories in particular appear to have a direct link to flexibility. These are Central Coherence and Executive Function.

Central Coherence theory

The Central Coherence theory was first proposed by Uta Frith in 1989. Difficulties with central coherence in autism are characterised by 'a specific imbalance in integration of information at different levels' (Happé 1994, p.116) or weak central coherence. 'Normal' processing of information is said to be 'global', that is when bits of information are drawn together or integrated to form a whole picture (i.e. getting the gist). Those with weak central coherence on the other hand have a tendency towards 'local' information processing, taking bits of information piece by piece. This is often described as not being able to see the wood for the trees or as having a particular attention to detail to the exclusion of the bigger picture.

An analogy would be the gradual building of a picture of an animal – say a fox – by presenting it piece by piece (the ears, the legs, the body, etc.). Gradually those with good central coherence would collect and put the pieces together in their mind until they had enough information to identify the animal as a fox. Those with weak central coherence would take each piece of the picture as a separate item without seeing the links and then either not make the connection that it was a fox or take much longer to do so.

Difficulties with central coherence can therefore lead to:

- difficulties in seeing the whole or bigger picture, that is, in integrating pieces of information to get a wider picture

- extreme attention to detail

- selectivity or narrow focus

- difficulty in taking account of context (the bigger picture) to aid understanding

- difficulty with the interpretation of ambiguous language or absurdities

- difficulty with making connections or semantic links

- seeing life experiences as a succession of isolated incidences and not as one continuing or evolving process (i.e. not building on experience).

Looking at the list above, it is easy to see how some of the problems commonly associated with flexibility as set out earlier in the chapter could be linked to weak central coherence. If you have a narrow view of how things should be or look, this can lead to insistence on things needing to be the *same* (e.g. chairs, food, toilet, routines) or insistence on seeing something through despite situations changing. In other words it may lead to rigid and *inflexible* behaviour. If you see experiences as isolated incidences, this can lead to problems with generalising skills and using them functionally. Developing flexible thinking is therefore synonymous with the development of independence, in particular independence in thought which, in turn, allows independence in learning and independence in behaviour, especially in social situations.

However although weak central coherence can account for some of the difficulties commonly associated with poor flexibility, it does not account for them all. Poor executive function is increasingly being recognised as an underlying feature of poor flexibility.

Executive Function theory

Executive function, described as goal-directed behaviour or as the ability to problem solve and to plan, organise and think ahead, is often said to be impaired in individuals with autism. Executive *dysfunction* (or impaired executive function) is also a feature in several other disorders such as Attention Deficit Hyperactivity Disorder (ADHD) and Dyspraxia.

Executive function is an overall term used to describe the many different mental (or cognitive) processes that individuals use to control and regulate their behaviour and to prepare their response or action. This includes the process of making connections with past experiences and using this information to inform what you do next.

Executive functioning involves the planning, organising and sequencing needed to get to where you want to go or do what you want to do. This also includes planning and organising motor skills and physical actions. It involves monitoring and analysing how things are going and adapting accordingly. In other words, 'think, plan, do and review'.

Executive function also involves the use of the working memory, in particular the component known as the central executive (Baddeley 1986), described as a flexible system that is responsible for overall control of the working memory system. This includes selecting or ignoring information, storing information, retrieving information from long-term memory, switching attention between tasks and so forth. Recent research appears to indicate that rather than there being one main 'central' executive, there may be separate executive functions which work independently and can be affected differently.

Difficulties with executive function can have a significant impact on an individual's ability to work, learn and behave effectively and independently and can lead to:

- poor organisation and sequencing

- difficulty in planning and carrying out tasks

- difficulty with problem solving

- difficulty controlling attention

- difficulty controlling impulse

- difficulties with judging time and space

- difficulty adjusting or adapting learning or behaviour according to different demands.

The behaviour of individuals with poor executive function is as a consequence often rigid and inflexible (it is safer and easier to stick to what you know and usually do rather than try to work something out!). They can often be impulsive, having difficulty holding back responses and actions and not having the skills to think and plan before acting. They may have a large store of knowledge but have trouble applying this knowledge functionally and meaningfully (thinking, planning and doing!). They may often seem focused mainly on detail and have problems seeing the whole picture (similar to central coherence).

What then are the implications of flexibility difficulties for learning, social development, independence and behaviour?

Learning

Looking at the examples given in this chapter of the difficulties commonly associated with poor flexibility, it is easy to see how these could create barriers to learning, particularly to formal learning in a school setting. Here are some examples.

Having an extreme attention to detail and obsessive interests about a subject can be a strength in some circumstances. It offers an opportunity to develop factual knowledge to a level that might be difficult for some. However having detailed knowledge alone has a limited use unless you also have the ability to use this practically and functionally (which requires flexibility skills).

Having a rigid approach to learning may mean that you can only see or do things one way and do not have the flexibility to adapt your approach to a task or to think 'out of the box'. It may mean that you make only narrow choices of activities (always playing with the same toy in the same way) and this may prevent you from joining in with (and benefitting from) other learning opportunities offered.

Difficulties with generalisation may mean that although you learn a skill in one setting you may not automatically be able to use that skill in another setting (making connections). For example you may learn how to add and take away money in school but may not be able to work out how much change you get in a shop.

Difficulties with predicting and anticipating and with inference and deduction can all have a significant effect on a student's ability to understand and use information from a book or to answer reading comprehension questions.

Difficulties with flexibility create barriers to learning which are not always apparent, particularly when executive function or process is involved. For example the individual may appear to be very able, be able to talk about a subject in detail and answer questions about it. He or she may be able to read and to spell with ease, but when asked to write a page about the subject, produces work that appears to be well below what she or he is capable of. Is this student lazy? Careless? Lacking in motivation? The most likely explanation under these circumstances is that the executive function difficulties are creating a barrier. The task to be completed involves a number of processes, all of which need to be planned and organised and sequenced: think about the subject and the question posed, select the information you need, plan and organise the information in a coherent way, write it down (including organising it on the page, spelling, punctuation, etc.) and check it through. This is a difficult task for someone with executive function difficulties even without having to work alongside a group of other people who may be distracting. It is easy to see how this scenario can cause anxiety, frustration and upset and can lead to behaviour difficulties and work avoidance. The individual with flexibility difficulties will not just 'learn' the skills she or he needs. There is a need to offer support and skill training to ensure that she or he reaches their potential. How? This is addressed later in this book using the 5P Approach to Flexibility.

Play and social development

It isn't only learning that is affected by poor flexibility. Difficulties with flexibility affect our ability to develop play skills, to learn and use social skills and to develop relationships with others. For example, if your approach to play is rigid and repetitive and your interests narrow, your ability to explore the toys and activities around you and learn new skills and knowledge from these (exploratory play) will be limited. If you are not able to make connections and bring things together, see the bigger picture, this hampers your ability to build and construct and join things together to make new or more complex things (constructive play). If you are not able to look back at previous experiences, make connections to current experiences and use these in your play (symbolic play) or adapt these to create new activities and ideas, then your ability to develop imaginative or creative play will be restricted.

Similarly poor flexibility will affect an individual's ability to develop social play skills, social skills and relationships with others. If you are not good at anticipating or predicting what others may do, do not make the link with what you do and how someone reacts (seeing the whole picture), have difficulties planning, organising and sequencing the way you approach and interact with someone (you just react without thinking), this will affect the way you interact with others, your ability to share attention, to understand others and adapt your behaviour accordingly.

Many individuals with poor flexibility skills may be able to learn the social rules and how to apply them to social situations but their flexibility difficulties mean that they are then not able to adapt and apply the skills they have learned flexibly to suit the situation. This can lead to misunderstanding and confusion and at times may give the impression of rudeness (for example not changing or differentiating between the way you approach and interact with your friend, your parent, your teacher, etc.).

Independence – problem solving

One of the most important skills which flexible thinking brings is the ability to problem solve. Problem solving (of all kinds) is a complex process which requires highly flexible thinking. Problem solving involves thinking about 'why' and 'how', it involves making choices, decisions and plans. To be able to problem solve is a key skill which gives us independence in thought, learning and behaviour.

We encounter problems in every aspect of our lives, from simple problems (which we often don't even recognise as being problems) to more complex academic problems and in social problem solving. Problems we encounter can be placed broadly into four main categories:

- Social or emotional problems.

  How to ask? How to play? What should I do when? What should I say when?

- Academic or intellectual problems.

  What to use? Where to find? How to do? Problem solving.

- Every day issues.

  What to wear? What to eat? What to play with? What to do with my time?

- Physical problems.

  Where to sit? Where to find? Where to go and how to get there, physical proximity, physical (motor) routines.

In order to problem solve one needs a sense of purpose, to be goal orientated, to know what the end point should be and to flexibly apply strategies. It involves trying things out and adapting approaches to gain success. One also needs to be able to evaluate the efficiency and effectiveness of the problem-solving strategies chosen and used.

The skills needed for problem solving can therefore all clearly be linked to flexible thinking. Is it any wonder that this is an area so many children and young people with flexibility difficulties find hard? Problem solving is examined further later in this book along with some practical strategies that can be used to support developing problem-solving skills.

The elements of flexibility

In summary, flexibility is a complex and multifaceted area. It has its roots in the way we process information, plan and organise and use our skills functionally. To be a flexible thinker we have to be adaptable and creative. Without flexibility we may become rigid and narrow in our approach.

This chapter has provided an overview of flexibility and its origins and has given a number of examples of how this manifests in those who present with flexibility difficulties. Flexibility of thought touches several areas of development and skill which often interrelate. The first step in supporting individuals to develop flexibility skills is to identify their strengths and difficulties. The 5P Approach to Flexibility provides a framework for doing this, beginning with an outline of the flexibility 'elements', those areas which require flexibility skills and which most often occur as barriers to learning or are commonly associated with behaviour issues. Figure 1.1 sets out the 5P Approach to Flexibility: Elements of Flexibility.

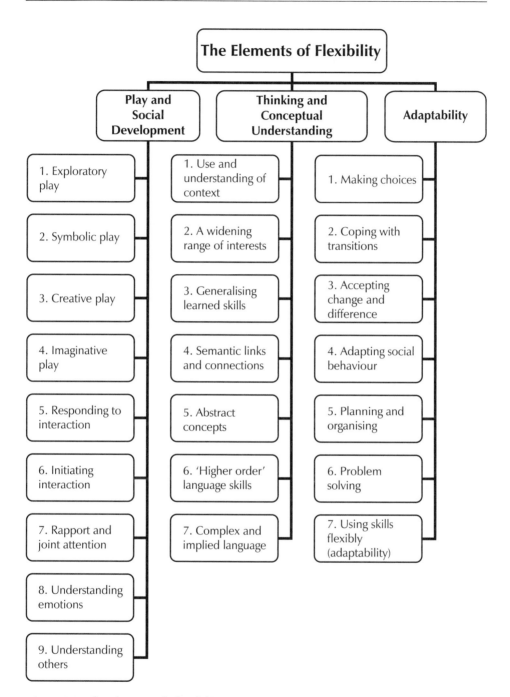

Figure 1.1: The Elements of Flexibility

What about behaviour?

There are numerous examples within this chapter of how poor flexibility skills may lead to behaviour issues. Whether behaviour issues arise through lack of skills, through anxiety, anger or frustration or a lack of understanding or misunderstanding, the most important thing to remember is that behaviour which has poor flexibility as its underlying cause will not simply improve without some specific intervention and support.

Any behaviour challenge which arises should be carefully examined to find the root cause or function of the behaviour. Once this has been established, the next step is to create a positive and preventative intervention plan which includes creating an environment which supports the individual and addresses any flexibility issues, the teaching and reinforcement of new skills, the teaching of coping strategies (while new skills develop) and a plan of how to react to a challenging behaviour when it occurs.

The 5P Approach, introduced in my last book, *Practical Behaviour Management Solutions for Children and Teens with Autism – The 5P Approach,* provides a comprehensive and practical framework which can be used by professionals, parents and organisations who want a better understanding of behaviour, how to prevent issues arising and how to manage behaviour change. The 5P Approach promotes 'GREEN' behaviour intervention. At its core is a focus on prevention (being in the GREEN Zone) rather than 'cure'. It uses the distinctive GREEN, AMBER and RED traffic light colours to distinguish between levels of behaviour and places the emphasis on using different strategies at the different levels.

The 5P Approach to Flexibility uses these principles and builds upon this philosophy. With a focus on prevention, it looks at how the 5P Approach can be applied to issues specific to flexibility.

References

American Pyschiatric Association (1994) *Diagnostic and Statistical Manual of Mental Disorders* 4th Edition. Washington, DC: APA.

Baddeley, A. D. (1986) *Working Memory.* Oxford: Oxford University Press.

Baron-Cohen, S. and Swettenham, J. (1997) 'Theory of Mind in Autism: Its Relationship to Executive Function and Central Coherence.' In D. Cohen and F. Volkmar (eds) *Handbook of Autism and Pervasive Developmental Disorders* 2nd Edition. Chichester: John Wiley and Sons.

Happé, F. (1994) *Autism: An Introduction to Psychological Theory.* London: UCL Press Ltd.

Miller, L. (2009) *Practical Behaviour Management Solutions for Children and Teens with Autism – The 5P Approach.* London and Philadelphia: Jessica Kingsley Publishers.

National Institute for Health and Clinical Excellence (NICE) (2011) *NICE Clinical Guideline 128. Autism: Recognition, Referral and Diagnosis of Children and Young People on the Autism Spectrum.* London: NICE Publications.

Ozanoff, S. (1995) 'Executive Function in Autism.' In E. Schopler and G. Mesibov (eds) *Learning and Cognition in Autism.* New York: Plenum Press.

Wing, L. and Gould, J. (1979) 'Severe impairments of social interaction and associated abnormalities in children: Epidemiology and classification.' *Journal of Autism and Developmental Disorders* 9, 11–29.

World Health Organization (WHO) (1992) *International Classification of Diseases* 10th Edition. Geneva: WHO.

Chapter 2

WHAT CAN WE DO TO HELP?

Introducing the 5P Approach to Flexibility

The 5P Approach and flexibility

As described at the end of the previous chapter the 5P Approach, characterised by its distinct traffic light colours, provides a complete framework for behaviour intervention which has its roots in prevention and good practice. It places an emphasis on promoting and encouraging the development of skills and independence, through using the 5Ps – Profiling, Prioritising, Problem analysis, Problem solving and Planning. So how does this link to flexibility?

The 5P Approach to behaviour intervention places an emphasis on prevention and problem solving. It is built upon the philosophy that understanding *why* particular behaviours occur is the key to successful prevention and intervention. We have already seen that issues relating to flexibility can be very common causes of behaviour problems in children and young people with autism and other disorders. But while there is no doubt that flexibility has a huge impact on behaviour, in my experience it is often the area that is least talked about in terms of prevention. The development of flexibility or addressing a flexibility issue is often found within behaviour management programmes (reacting to a problem) rather than within a specialist curriculum or individual learning programme (preventing and pre-empting a problem). In other words, the emphasis is often on reacting to the effects of poor flexibility rather than on the teaching of flexibility skills. The 5P Approach to Flexibility sets out therefore to raise awareness about the importance of flexibility and to look at where it fits with planning and intervention.

The 5P Approach, with its solution-focused, preventative emphasis, ensures that any strategies used for intervention quickly become part of a general preventative approach and that these are established as part of the foundations (known as being in the GREEN!) which are created to prevent issues from arising and provide the optimum environment for learning. It has a clear five step pathway to support movement from RED to GREEN when a challenging behaviour occurs and to support the development of overall good practice (GREEN). The 5P Approach principles, the process and pathway (Profile, Prioritise, Problem analyse, Problem solve and Plan) can be used equally effectively when the focus is specifically on flexibility.

The 5P Approach to Flexibility, as with the 5P Approach to behaviour intervention, places a focus on developing skills and creating foundations (the GREEN Zone) which prevent behaviour issues from arising and support the development of independence. Establishing GREEN strategies and a GREEN environment are particularly important for the area of flexibility and this book sets out to show how this can be done.

Using the principles and philosophy of the 5P Approach, the 5P Approach to Flexibility also uses the distinct RED, AMBER and GREEN traffic light colours to outline a flexibility framework which addresses how to identify what flexibility skills an individual has and what skills they need to develop, how to create an environment which reduces stress and uses best practice strategies (GREEN) and how to deal with and learn from any issues that may arise.

In the 5P Approach to Flexibility, there are four key intervention strands which work together and alongside the 5P Approach to behaviour intervention. These are set out in Figure 2.1.

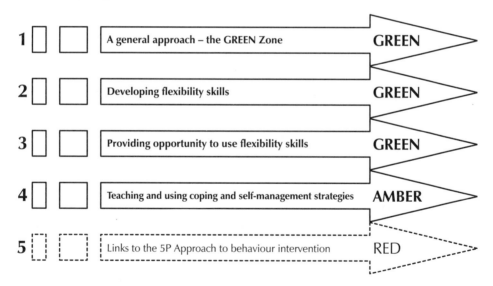

Figure 2.1: The 5P Approach Flexibility Strands

About the four strands

1. The general intervention approach – creating the GREEN Zone

   This involves planning the general approach which works with the individual's learning style and creating a safe environment in which the individual can learn and interact (and so reducing stress).

2. Developing flexibility skills (GREEN)

   This involves supporting the individual to develop the skills needed to improve flexibility of thought and move further towards independence.

3. Providing opportunities to develop flexibility (GREEN)

   Provide or organise opportunities specifically designed to make use of and generalise developing flexible thinking skills.

4. Teaching coping and self-management strategies (AMBER)

   Support the individual to use strategies which act as coping or self-management strategies. These are those which reduce anxiety and provide a means of increasing flexibility while new skills develop.

Dealing with RED – the fifth strand

When poor flexibility leads to difficulties with behaviour (i.e. going into the RED), the 5P Approach to behaviour intervention as set out in *Practical Behaviour Management Solutions for Children and Teens with Autism – The 5P Approach* is used to guide through the process of problem solving and creating an Intervention Hierarchy. To show this link with the wider 5P Approach, this fifth flexibility strand is represented on the Flexibility Strands diagram (Figure 2.1) in faint type.

In the 5P Approach, creating a positive and preventative intervention plan doesn't just involve working out how to deal with a troublesome RED behaviour, it involves planning RED, AMBER and GREEN strategies which work together and act as a whole plan for the individual. The 5P Approach identifies five elements which all play a crucial part in managing behaviour change and preventing issues from arising in the future. These are set out in Figure 2.2.

Because the 5P Approach philosophy has its roots in prevention, when working out why a RED behaviour has occurred, the focus is on planning what to do and what to put into place to prevent it from happening next time (learning from experience). This philosophy is reflected in the structure of the 5P Approach Intervention Hierarchy. Containing all the essential behaviour change elements, this is used as a quick reference to set out the plan to be used when a RED behaviour has been identified. A full version of the 5P Approach Intervention Hierarchy can be found in *Practical Behaviour Management Solutions for Children and Teens with Autism – The 5P Approach* or downloaded from the 5P Approach website. A summarised version can be found in Table 2.1.

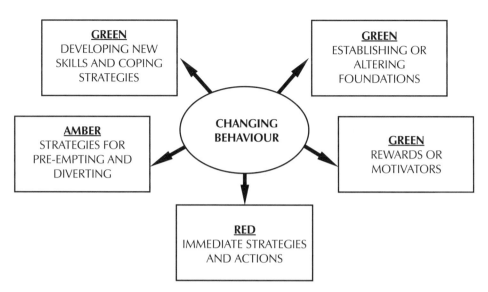

Figure 2.2: The 5P Approach Behaviour Change Elements

Table 2.1 The 5P Approach Intervention Hierarchy

The 5P Approach Intervention Hierarchy	What Behaviour?	What Strategy?
Red Level Not acceptable or over the top Clear signal of disapproval and consequence		
Amber Level 'Bubbling' behaviour (pre-cursors to more difficult behaviour) Pre-empt, divert and distract		
Green Level: GREEN ONE (Foundations – Good practice) Managing with everyday strategies		
Green Level: GREEN TWO Doing the right thing, doing well New skills and reward		

This whole process aims to prevent an individual from getting to RED (or dealing with RED as quickly as possible and moving back to GREEN). AMBER strategies are used to pre-empt or head off any behaviour once 'bubbling' signs emerge. As the use of AMBER coping strategies and new skills develop, they become part of the foundations or GREEN Zone, the GREEN expands and the number of RED behaviours reduces. This reflects a learning from experience philosophy. The process is shown in the 5P Approach intervention triangle (see Figure 2.3).

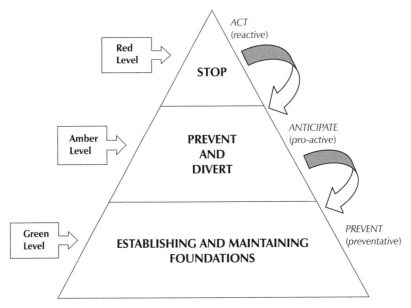

Figure 2.3: The 5P Approach Intervention Triangle

The 5P Approach to Flexibility

As we have seen in the previous chapter, poor flexibility or flexible thinking affects the development of a number of key skills in both learning and social development. The 5P Approach to Flexibility identifies three main elements (Figure 1.1): Play and Social Development, Thinking and Conceptual Understanding and Adaptability, all of which are affected in some way by poor flexibility and all of which create barriers to learning and social development and frequently lead to behaviour difficulties. However, although flexibility is an area of difficulty shared by all children and young people with autism, everyone is an individual. Not everyone has the same overall degree or range of problems in each of these flexibility areas. The 5P Approach to Flexibility therefore introduces the concept of a flexibility continuum. The use of a flexibility continuum reflects the differing levels of flexibility skill seen in individuals who experience difficulties in this area and also provides a way of demonstrating the development of flexibility skills. The 5P Approach Flexibility Continuum is set out in Table 2.2.

Table 2.2 The 5P Approach Flexibility Continuum

	LEVEL ONE	LEVEL TWO	LEVEL THREE	LEVEL FOUR	LEVEL FIVE
Teaching Approaches and Environment	Working with the learning style Creating a safe, structured environment for the reduction of stress	Teaching and developing coping strategies: A structured approach with some challenge and change and taught opportunity to use coping strategies	Teaching and developing new skills: A structured approach with some challenge and change and opportunity to use newly developing skills	Providing opportunities for generalisation of skills taught and learned: A less structured and predictable approach	Providing opportunities for problem solving and independence: Minimal structure, maximum opportunity for independent thinking and behaviour
Degree of flexibility	Rigid/inflexible in behaviour and learning (Narrow focus and interests)	Use of strategies (taught or self developed) to *cope* successfully with change, choice or challenge	Developing new skills in flexibility (e.g. tolerance, making choices and decisions, problem solving, understanding abstract concepts, etc.)	Using newly acquired skills in different situations with prompt (e.g. generalisation, adaptability, problem solving) *Demonstrated in learning and behaviour*	Acquired independence in thought. No or minimal prompts needed *Demonstrated in learning and behaviour*
Level of Independence	Fully supported and mainly passive in interaction Low level of independence	Partially supported/ partial independence *Using coping strategies*	Partially supported/ partial independence *Developing new skills*	Independent *With minimal external support or prompt*	Fully independent *May use self-prompt strategies*

This continuum plots the development of flexible thinking through five levels from, at the lowest level (Level 1), a rigid and inflexible approach in behaviour and learning, through to the acquisition of new skills in flexibility and acquired independence in thought (Level 5). The flexibility levels and descriptors can be seen in the shaded area across the middle of the table (the degree of flexibility).

To ensure that we support the development and functional use of flexibility skills, the environment, strategies and approaches (i.e. the GREEN Zone) should match an individual's level of flexibility. If we don't do this, and instead for example maintain a rigid and over structured approach to teaching when an individual has learned the flexibility skills they need to enable them to work and play within a less structured environment, we could be preventing them from making progress and preventing the development of independence. The levels of the 5P Flexibility Continuum are therefore also linked to the type of approach used (seen at the top of the table). As an individual moves along the continuum, the type of approach and environment will also change to keep in step with this progress.

Similarly the level of flexibility of an individual will have a bearing on their level of independence which again should improve as functional use of flexibility skills develops (seen at the bottom of the table).

Where do we start?

The first thing to do is to set about creating a plan using all four strands of the 5P Approach to Flexibility i.e. creating the GREEN Zone, developing skills (GREEN), teaching coping or self-management strategies (AMBER) and providing opportunities to develop flexibility (GREEN). Before we can do any of this, however, we need to assess exactly what skills a child or young person already has (which indicates what type of approaches we should be thinking about using) and which skills she or he needs to develop (which not only indicates what any future targets should be but also what coping strategies might be needed while new skills are developing). Establishing a method of flexibility assessment is therefore an essential first step. The 5P Approach to Flexibility introduces a unique and comprehensive assessment tool, the 5P Approach Flexibility Assessment, which provides a means of assessing flexibility skills and measuring small step progress. This is introduced in the next chapter.

References

Miller, L. (2009) *Practical Behaviour Management Solutions for Children and Teens with Autism – The 5P Approach*. London and Philadelphia: Jessica Kingsley Publishers.
Website: www.5papproach.co.uk

Chapter 3

THE 5P APPROACH FLEXIBILITY ASSESSMENT

This 5P Approach Flexibility Assessment has evolved over a number of years and has been trialled by a number of professionals in schools and provisions. The assessment plays a key role in any flexibility curriculum or flexibility intervention plan. It offers a basis for formative (gradually over time) and summative (at the beginning or end of a period of time) assessment of flexibility skills and provides a means of identifying targets and monitoring progress within a specific area (flexibility) which is often not included as a separate area within traditional school based or clinical assessments.

The 5P Approach Flexibility Assessment, used in conjunction with the other materials from the 5P Approach, provides a toolkit which helps to identify priorities and informs the type of intervention and strategies required. As described in the previous chapter, this assessment tool can also be used to support the 5P Approach problem-solving stage when behaviour issues arise.

Using the Flexibility Elements set out in Figure 1.1, a range of skills commonly associated with flexible thinking is identified. Flexibility skill development is then measured in two dimensions: a within-skill assessment (graded from 1: not present to 5: established) and a move along the flexibility continuum ranging from Level 1 (rigid and inflexible behaviour and learning) to Level 5 (acquired independence in thought).

The 5P Approach Flexibility Assessment comprises:

- The Flexibility Checklist

- The Individual Flexibility Continuum

- The Flexibility Target Sheet.

The Flexibility Checklist

The Flexibility Checklist can be found in Table 3.1. It comprises three elements (as set out in Figure 1.1) which represent three main skill areas associated with flexibility of thought:

- play and social development

- thinking and conceptual understanding

- adaptability.

Assessment

As set out in the introduction, the Flexibility Checklist provides a means of recording skills on a scale of 1–5. The aim is to record only skills and progress which are persistent and demonstrated over time rather than information simply obtained from a one off assessment or observation. Completion of this checklist is therefore best done through a range of methods, by someone who knows the child or young person well or in discussion with those who do, through a series of observations and through use of specifically planned activities which prompt the use of flexibility skills. The assessment activity and resources section found within Table 3.5: Recording Flexibility Observations and Skill Achievement provides information on how this can be done. However, if planned activities are used for this purpose, it is important to ensure that any conclusion drawn reflects established or persistent use of skills rather than a single success or failure (see Score Descriptors, Table 3.4).

Table 3.1 The Flexibility Checklist

Pupil Name:

Date/s completed:

Play and social development

Skill		Assessed level of development				Example: How does s/he show this? (Please note scoring should be based on persistent behaviour over time rather than single observation)	Person/s contributing to assessment
		B	T1	T2	T3		
1	No exploratory play, few repetitive actions only						
1a	Limited exploratory play, mainly self-interested						
1b	Shows exploratory play but within a narrow range of activities/interests only						
1c	Shows exploratory play across a wide range of activities/interests						
2	Shows symbolic play using a small range of copied routines/actions						
2a	Engages in symbolic play using a wide range of actions/activities						
2b	Use of symbolic play is spontaneous and varied						
3	Demonstrates constructive creative play (solitary) (e.g. joining bricks, combining toys)						
3a	Engages in constructive creative play (as above) with adult (e.g. joint tower building, creating train track, etc.)						
3b	Engages in constructive creative play (as above) with peer (e.g. joint tower building, creating train track, etc.)						
3c	Engages in constructive creative play within a small group						
	Sub-total						

continued

Skill		Assessed level of development				Example: How does s/he show this? (Please note scoring should be based on persistent behaviour over time rather than single observation)	Person/s contributing to assessment
		B	T1	T2	T3		
	Sub-total carried forward						
4	Engages in imaginative play (solitary) (i.e. creates new and original play routines)						
4a	Engages in imaginative play with adult						
4b	Engages in imaginative play with peer						
4c	Engages in imaginative play within a group (i.e. role play)						
5	Responds to ADULT initiating interaction (acknowledges non-verbally e.g. eye contact, facial expression)						
5a	Responds to ADULT initiating interaction by responding physically (e.g. touching, moving toward person, etc.)						
5b	Responds to ADULT initiating interaction by responding verbally (sounds or words)						
5c	Responds to PEER initiating interaction (acknowledges non verbally (e.g. eye contact, facial expression)						
5d	Responds to PEER initiating interaction by responding physically (e.g. touching, moving toward person, etc.)						
5e	Responds to PEER initiating interaction by responding verbally (sounds or words)						
6	Initiating interaction with ADULT physically (i.e. by touch/approach, etc.)						
6a	Initiating interaction with ADULT non-verbally (i.e. eye contact, facial expression, gesture, etc.)						
	Sub-total						

Skill	Assessed level of development				Example: How does s/he show this? (Please note scoring should be based on persistent behaviour over time rather than single observation)	Person/s contributing to assessment
	B	T1	T2	T3		
Sub-total carried forward						
6b Initiating interaction with ADULT verbally (using sound or word)						
6c Initiating interaction with PEER physically (i.e. by touch/approach, etc.)						
6d Initiating interaction with PEER non-verbally (i.e. eye contact, facial expression, gesture, etc.)						
6e Initiating interaction with PEER verbally (using sound or word)						
7 Developing rapport and joint attention with other – fleeting (less than 30 secs)						
7a Maintaining joint attention (1–2 mins)						
7b Sustaining joint attention (3 mins plus)						
7c Shows an ability to share interests with others (e.g. by pointing, drawing attention to something, etc).						
7d Demonstrates an ability to share interests with others with a shared experience (e.g. book)						
8 Is able to identify and label (verbal or non-verbal) a small range of emotions from photos, pictures, etc.						
8a Is able to identify and label (verbal or non-verbal) a wide range of emotions from photos, pictures, etc.						
8b Shows an ability to identify/recognise emotions in others (by verbal or non-verbal means)						
Sub-total						

continued

Skill		Assessed level of development				Example: How does s/he show this? (Please note scoring should be based on persistent behaviour over time rather than single observation)	Person/s contributing to assessment
		B	T1	T2	T3		
	Sub-total carried forward						
8c	Shows an ability to identify emotions in self (by use of sign, symbol or word, etc.)						
8d	Responds to the emotions of others (verbally or non-verbally/behaviourally) (i.e. changes behaviour)						
8e	Shows an understanding of the emotions of others (empathy) (e.g. by touching someone crying)						
8f	Shows an understanding of the emotions of others (empathy) and acts accordingly (e.g. by offering support)						
9	Has an understanding that others have differing points of view (i.e. not everyone thinks the same)						
9a	Shows an acceptance of another's point of view (e.g. tolerance, will accept their way of doing something, etc.)						
	TOTAL	205	205	205	205		

	OVERALL LEVEL DESCRIPTOR:	B	T1	T2	T3
	LEVEL				

Totals	Level Descriptor
41 → 77	Level One
78 → 114	Level Two
115 → 151	Level Three
152 → 188	Level Four
189 → 205	Level Five

Assessment description	Score
Not present	1
Emerging skills	2
Developing skills	3
Using new skills	4
Established	5

Thinking skills and conceptual understanding

Skill	Assessed level of development				Example: How does s/he show this? (Please note scoring should be based on persistent behaviour over time rather than single observation)	Person/s contributing to assessment
	B	T1	T2	T3		
1	An ability to take account of context to aid understanding in *practical* activities (e.g. puzzle completion)					
1a	An ability to take account of context to aid understanding in learning (e.g. understanding a story)					
1b	Ability to take account of context to aid understanding in social situations (e.g. awareness of situation)					
1c	Ability to grasp the bigger picture, to have an overview (i.e. sees the whole picture and takes it into account)					
2	A small range of interests/toys/activities (5+)					
2a	A developing range of interests/toys/activities (10+)					
2b	A wide and varied range of interests					
3	An ability to generalise learned skills across people					
3a	An ability to generalise learned skills across environments					
3b	An ability to generalise learned skills across situations					
4	An understanding of categories and 'families' (semantic links) (i.e. knows how things relate to one another)					
4a	An understanding of similarities between people, objects and things (semantic links) (i.e. in what way things are the same)					
Sub-total						

continued

The SP Approach

Skill		Assessed level of development				Example: How does s/he show this? (Please note scoring should be based on persistent behaviour over time rather than single observation)	Person/s contributing to assessment
		B	T1	T2	T3		
	Sub-total carried forward						
4b	An ability to make connections with previous experiences (i.e. think back to previous events)						
5	An understanding of abstract concepts (simple) (e.g. time)						
5a	An understanding of abstract concepts (complex) (e.g. emotions, morality, etc).						
6	An ability to predict in learning (i.e. what happens next)						
6a	An ability to predict in people (i.e. what they are going to do)						
6b	An ability to predict in social settings (i.e what happens next)						
6c	An ability to make deductions in learning (i.e. using knowledge to work out an answer or what to do next)						
6d	An ability to make deductions in social situations, (i.e. to work out an answer or what to do next)						
6e	An understanding of *implied* meaning or inference (e.g. aren't you cold without a coat?)						
7	An understanding of informal language or slang expressions (e.g. cut it out, take this chair, etc.)						
7a	An understanding of jokes, sarcasm and humour						
7b	An understanding of homonyms, metaphors and similes (e.g. he ran like the wind, the moon sailed across the sky, pins and needles, etc.)						
	TOTAL	120	120	120	120	OVERALL LEVEL DESCRIPTOR:	B	T1	T2	T3
						LEVEL	

Copyright © Linda Miller 2013

Assessment description	Score
Not present	1
Emerging skills	2
Developing skills	3
Using new skills	4
Established	5

Totals	Level Descriptor
24 → 43	Level One
44 → 63	Level Two
64 → 83	Level Three
84 → 103	Level Four
104 → 120	Level Five

Adaptability

Skill		Assessed level of development				Example: How does s/he show this? (Please note scoring should be based on persistent behaviour over time rather than single observation)	Person/s contributing to assessment
		B	T1	T2	T3		
1	An ability to make choices: needs led (e.g. drink, food)						
1a	An ability to make choices: preferences/likes (e.g. choice of toys, videos, etc)						
1b	An ability to make choices in social situations (e.g. who to speak to, when to walk away, etc.)						
1c	An ability to make simple choices in learning (e.g. art materials, books, colours, etc.)						
1d	An ability to make complex choices in learning (e.g. strategies, options)						
	Sub-total						

continued

The 5P Approach

Skill	Assessed level of development				Example: How does s/he show this? (Please note scoring should be based on persistent behaviour over time rather than single observation)	Person/s contributing to assessment
	B	T1	T2	T3		
Sub-total carried forward						
2 An ability to cope with 'macro' transitions (e.g. life and big events)						
2a An ability to cope with 'mezzo' transitions (e.g. to different areas/across environments)						
2b An ability to cope with 'micro' transitions (e.g. within and between activities)						
3 An acceptance of change to routine or structure						
3a An acceptance of change to rules and procedures						
3b An ability to cope with sudden change, unpredictability and novel activities						
3c An ability to accept and cope successfully with differing approaches to learning/tasks						
4 An ability to adapt social behaviour to differing situations (e.g. being quiet in the library)						
4a An understanding of social hierarchy (e.g. the difference between a friend, a teacher and a parent)						
4b An understanding of social hierarchy and an ability to adapt behaviour accordingly						
5 Organisation and planning skills: personal (e.g. dressing, self-care, possessions, etc.)						
Sub-total						

Copyright © Linda Miller 2013

Skill	Assessed level of development				Example: How does s/he show this? (Please note scoring should be based on persistent behaviour over time rather than single observation)	Person/s contributing to assessment
	B	T1	T2	T3		
Sub-total carried forward						
5a	Organisation and planning skills in learning (planning, sequencing, carrying out a task)					
5b	Organisation and planning skills in social situations (e.g. planning social outcomes, games, etc.)					
6	Early problem-solving skills: trial and error (practical)					
6a	An ability to identify and apply rules in learning (used to problem solve): practical (e.g. put tops on felt tips, the big bricks go on the bottom, etc.)					
6b	An ability to identify and apply rules in learning (used to problem solve) – simple starting writing on the left, etc.					
6c	An ability to identify and apply rules in learning (used to problem solve) – complex (e.g. always add the units first)					
6d	Identifying and applying rules in social situations: practical (e.g. if you go in the rain you get wet, ask for help)					
6e	Identifying and applying rules in social situations: simple (e.g. walk on the pavement, follow teacher's instructions, playground games, etc.)					
6f	Identifying and applying rules in social situations – complex (e.g. don't talk to strangers, offer help to a friend in trouble, etc.)					
6g	Identifying and applying rules in dealing with everyday situations – practical (e.g. socks before shoes)					
Sub-total						

continued

Skill	Assessed level of development				Example: How does s/he show this? (Please note scoring should be based on persistent behaviour over time rather than single observation)	Person/s contributing to assessment
	B	T1	T2	T3		
Sub-total carried forward						
6h	Identifying and applying rules in dealing with everyday situations – complex (e.g. if you miss a bus wait for the next, etc.)					
7	An ability to transfer learned skills to new situations (generalisation and flexible use): learning situations					
7a	An ability to use learned life skills functionally					
7b	An ability to transfer learned skills to new situations (generalisation and flexible use): across people					
7c	An ability to transfer learned skills to new situations (generalisation and flexible use): across environments					
TOTAL	155	155	155	155		

OVERALL LEVEL DESCRIPTOR:

	B	T1	T2	T3
LEVEL				

Totals	Level Descriptor
31 → 57	Level One
58 → 84	Level Two
85 → 111	Level Three
112 → 136	Level Four
137 → 155	Level Five

Assessment description	Score
Not present	1
Emerging skills	2
Developing skills	3
Using new skills	4
Established	5

Getting started

In order to monitor progress, the checklist has capacity for baseline and termly assessment. Scores for each time period are recorded in B, T1, T2 and T3.

The first step is to provide a baseline. Each of the three flexibility elements is scored separately. Each element comprises several statements describing behaviour which represents a flexibility skill. Different skills are numbered 1, 2, 3, etc. Progression within skills is broadly developmental with stages sub-labelled a, b, c, etc. For example, the first skill for Play and Social Development: Exploratory Play, includes statements 1, 1a, 1b, 1c and 1d in developmental order. Each statement is then given a score of 1–5 (not present – established) in the assessed level of development column according to the level of skill development to date (see Table 3.2).

Table 3.2 Scoring Key

Description	Score
Not present	1
Emerging	2
Developing new skills	3
Using new skills	4
Established	5

The decision to use a 1–5 scoring system and the others in this book rather than using 0–4 reflects the view that all individuals have a degree of skill development however severe their needs present.

When scoring skill areas, *all* developmental statements must be scored. If skills are already present these are scored at 5. In some instances, as in the Play and Social Development element, the term 'established' should also be read as 'exceeded' and scored as 5. For example for item 1a, the statement 'no exploratory play' should be scored at 5 if the child has passed or exceeded this stage of development.

A sub-total for each element is calculated and recorded at the bottom of the column on each page and brought forward to the top of the next page. The total score for each element is calculated at the end of that section of the checklist. This is then converted to element Level Descriptors using the key provided. For example, the Level Descriptors for the element Play and Social Development can be seen in Table 3.3.

Table 3.3 Level Descriptors Example for Play and Social Development Element

Totals	Level descriptor
41 → 77	Level One
78 → 114	Level Two
115 → 151	Level Three
152 → 188	Level Four
189 → 205	Level Five

Score Descriptors

Rating skill development on a scale of 1–5 is of course subjective and reliant on an individual's interpretation and understanding of the child or young person. In order to maintain consistency in recording the guidance in Table 3.4 sets out some broad criteria upon which judgements can be made.

Table 3.4 Score Descriptors

Score	Descriptor	Criteria
1	Not present	As stated. Skill not present, never observed
2	Emerging skill	Partially developed skill observed (i.e. just beginning). Seen infrequently (less than 1 × weekly) requires very high level of prompt and support
3	Developing skill	Skill observed more frequently (min 2–3 × weekly). Requires lower level of prompt and support. Occasional spontaneous use
4	Using new skill	Skill observed on a frequent basis (min 3–5 × weekly) requiring little prompt. Skill used *functionally* (sometimes with reminders/prompt) sometimes spontaneously
5	Established	Skill used independently and spontaneously within a range of settings. No prompts or support required

Recording observations and skill achievement

The Flexibility Checklist also has a section for recording an example or behaviour description of how the child or young person displays that she or he has acquired the skill recorded (how does s/he show this?). This section should be completed when a score of 5 is given, thus giving a concrete example of how the skill has been demonstrated. For best practice, skill acquisition can also be recorded through photo or video which is cross referenced under the relevant item.

Examples of what type of skill or behaviour would be observed when an individual has achieved a score of 5 for each of the statements in the Flexibility Checklist can be found in Table 3.5.

Table 3.5 Recording Flexibility Observations and Skill Achievement

The *Flexibility Checklist* also has a section for recording an example of how the child or young person displays that s/he has acquired the skill. This should be completed when a score of 5 is given, giving a concrete example of how the skill has been demonstrated. For best practice, skill acquisition can also be recorded through photo or video which is cross referenced under the relevant item.

Examples of what type of skill or behaviour would be observed for each of the statements in the *Flexibility Checklist* are set out below.

ELEMENT: PLAY AND SOCIAL DEVELOPMENT

Skill		Example: How would s/he show this?
1	No exploratory play, few repetitive actions only	Play tends to be repetitive and stereotyped (e.g. repeatedly tipping bricks, spinning objects, flapping paper, etc.) with little variety
1a	Limited exploratory play, mainly self-interested	Drawn to a few (1–3) favoured items only. Explores with senses (touch, taste, smell, etc.). Play still mostly repetitive in nature
1b	Shows exploratory play but within a narrow range of activities/interests only	Explores using senses, moves towards and between different objects and spends time with each. Limited range (5–10 items)
1c	Shows exploratory play across a wide range of activities/interests	As above but moves freely around the environment exploring a wide range of items. Drawn to unfamiliar items and shows curiosity
2	Shows symbolic play using a small range of copied routines/actions	Demonstrates simple play routines which are always identical (e.g. stirring with a spoon, pushing a car, brushing doll's hair) and with no variation
2a	Engages in symbolic play using a wide range of actions/activities	Has acquired several learned symbolic actions including sequences (e.g. pouring tea into a cup, brushing floor and tipping rubbish into a bin, putting baby to bed, etc.)
2b	Use of symbolic play is spontaneous and varied	Demonstrates a wide range of symbolic actions which vary in length and complexity
3	Demonstrates constructive creative play (solitary) (i.e. joining bricks, combining toys)	Builds a tower, put bricks into a tractor, creates a train track, etc.
3a	Engages in constructive creative play (as above) with adult (e.g. joint tower building, creating train track, etc.)	Will take turns and/or build alongside an adult even if not engaging in any other interaction

continued

Skill		Example: How would s/he show this?
3b	Engages in constructive creative play (as above) with peer (e.g. joint tower building, creating train track, etc.)	As above with peer
3c	Engages in constructive creative play within a small group	As above with small group of peers (2+)
4	Engages in imaginative play (solitary) (i.e. creates NEW and original play routines)	Play shows signs of newly created or changing routines – natural and spontaneous
4a	Engages in imaginative play with adult	Will engage an adult in play routine (e.g. giving a cup of tea) or responds to adult initiated play routine and persists with play sequence
4b	Engages in imaginative play with peer	As above with peer
4c	Engages in imaginative play within a group (i.e. role play)	As above with small peer group (2+). Takes on a role (e.g. the baby, a fireman, etc.)
5	Responds to ADULT initiating interaction (acknowledges non-verbally e.g. eye contact, facial expression)	Immediate positive response to adult initiated interaction which indicates acknowledgement
5a	Responds to ADULT initiating interaction by responding physically (e.g. touching, moving toward person, etc.)	As above. Engages physically in play
5b	Responds to ADULT initiating interaction by responding verbally (sounds or words)	As above. Engages verbally in play
5c	Responds to PEER initiating interaction (acknowledges non-verbally (e.g. eye contact, facial expression)	As 5 above with peer
5d	Responds to PEER initiating interaction by responding physically (e.g. touching, moving toward person, etc.)	As 5a above with peer
5e	Responds to PEER initiating interaction by responding verbally (sounds or words)	As 5b above with peer
6	Initiating interaction with ADULT physically (i.e. by touch/approach, etc).	Actively moves towards adult with purpose of engaging/gaining attention by touching, etc.
6a	Initiating interaction with ADULT non-verbally (i.e. eye contact, facial expression, gesture, etc.)	As above non-verbally

Skill		Example: How would s/he show this?
6b	Initiating interaction with ADULT verbally (using sound or word)	As above verbally
6c	Initiating interaction with PEER physically (i.e. by touch/approach, etc.)	As 6 above with peer
6d	Initiating interaction with PEER non-verbally (i.e. eye contact, facial expression, gesture, etc.)	As 6a above with peer
6e	Initiating interaction with PEER verbally (using sound or word)	As 6b above with peer
7	Developing rapport and joint attention with other – fleeting (less than 30 secs)	Will share attention with adult or peer (e.g. looking at a toy, a book, a tickling game, etc.)
7a	Maintaining joint attention (1–2 mins)	As above 1–2 mins
7b	Sustaining joint attention (3 mins+)	As above 3 mins+
7c	Shows an ability to share interests with others (e.g. by pointing, drawing attention to something, etc.)	Draws another's interest to an object or person to engage them in sharing attention
7d	Demonstrates an ability to share interests with others with a shared experience (e.g. book)	Shares an experience with another (peer or adult), shows joint referencing (looking up and engaging another in the process e.g. pointing at a picture and looking up at the person or responding to an other)
8	Is able to identify and label (verbal or non-verbal) a small range of emotions from photos, pictures, etc.	Identifies and labels (using words, sign or pictures) 3–4 emotions (e.g. happy, sad, angry)
8a	Is able to identify and label (verbal or non-verbal) a wide range of emotions from photos, pictures, etc.	As above using a wider range of emotions (4+)
8b	Shows an ability to identify/recognise emotions in others (by verbal or non-verbal means)	Will *respond* to an other's expression of emotion (e.g. happy or sad) by labelling verbally or through sign or symbol
8c	Shows an ability to identify emotions in self (by use of sign, symbol or word, etc.)	Will say (verbally or non-verbally) I am sad, happy, etc. NB this must be in context and relevant not simply a choice of label
8d	Responds to the emotions of others (verbally or non-verbally/behaviourally) (i.e. changes behaviour	Will respond to recognising an other's emotion by a behaviour change (e.g. stops, looks, moves away, etc.)

continued

Skill		Example: How would s/he show this?
8e	Shows an understanding of the emotions of others (empathy) (e.g. by touching someone crying)	Demonstrates an understanding of an other's emotion by approaching, touching, facial expression of empathy, etc.
8f	Shows an understanding of the emotions of others (empathy) and acts accordingly (e.g. by offering support)	As above and also acts accordingly (e.g. hugs, gets a tissue, offers help, etc.)
9	Has an understanding that others have differing points of view (i.e. not everyone thinks the same)	Shows an understanding of the need to communicate a view (needs led or opinion) (i.e. does not expect someone to know what they want/feel/need)
9a	Shows an acceptance of another's point of view (e.g. tolerance, will accept their way of doing something, etc.)	Will accept that someone may do things differently and that this is (OK e.g. will take direction in play, follow a rule of a game, etc.) Will allow another to take control

Play and social development: Assessment activity and resources

This area is best assessed through observation, practical activity and interaction. Resources required include a range of play based materials:

- a range of toys including cause and effect, sensory and learning based toys
- a range of real and toy objects for symbolic and imaginative play routines such as cups, saucers, telephone, clothes, hats, etc.
- a range of constructive toys such as building bricks, train tracks, etc.
- books, photos and turn-taking and sharing activities such as balls, cars, etc.
- photos and symbols of emotions, books, stories and videos which contain emotions, etc.

Interaction based activities such as Intensive Interaction are also useful where the focus is on social interaction with adults.

ELEMENT: THINKING SKILLS AND CONCEPTUAL UNDERSTANDING

Skill		Example: How would s/he show this?
1	Shows an ability to take account of context to aid understanding in *practical* activities (e.g. puzzle completion)	Uses the bigger picture to help task completion (e.g. will find the missing wheel of a bus puzzle, will place the cow in the field, etc.)
1a	Shows an ability to take account of context to aid understanding in learning (e.g. understanding a story)	Can answer simple questions about a story (concrete)

Skill	Example: How would s/he show this?
1b	Shows an ability to take account of context to aid understanding in social situations (e.g. awareness of situation)	Will use information to make an assumption (e.g. taking cues from peers, when the bell rings it is the end of playtime and we all line up, we are quiet in a library, etc.)
1c	Shows an ability to grasp the bigger picture, to have an overview (i.e. sees the whole picture and takes it into account)	Will be able to guess/predict what happens next and react accordingly. Can answer more abstract questions about a story (e.g. if the girl has fallen in the picture she will be sad)
2	Has a small range of interests/toys/activities (5+)	Has a limited/narrow range of interests showing little interest in other experiences or activities presented and reluctance to move from preferred items.
2a	Has a developing range of interests/toys/activities (10+)	Shows a wider range of interests and will show some interest in other experiences and activities presented although tends to gravitate to move from preferred items
2b	Has a wide and varied range of interests	Has a wide range of interests and willing to take on new ideas and participate in new experiences
3	Shows an ability to generalise learned skills across people	Will use a skill learned in one context (e.g. saying hello) functionally with a number of adults, peers
3a	Shows an ability to generalise learned skills across environments	Will use a skill learned in one environment (e.g. dressing at home, functionally in another environment e.g. dressing at school, etc.)
3b	Shows an ability to generalise learned skills across situations	Will use a skill learned in one situation (e.g. problem solving (working out what to do) in a variety of situations, such as when and where to ask for help, etc.)
4	An understanding of categories and 'families' (semantic links) (i.e. knows how things relate to one another)	Is able to sort or label a variety of items into categories (e.g. farm animals, food, furniture, etc.)
4a	An understanding of similarities between people, objects and things (semantic links) (i.e. in what way things are the same)	Will show an understanding of how things can be the same but may look different (e.g. all knives are used for cutting, flowers may be different shapes, sizes and colours, people may be different shapes, sizes and colours, etc.)
4b	An ability to make connections with previous experiences (i.e. think back to previous events)	Will recall (verbally or with pictures) what happened when.

continued

Skill		Example: How would s/he show this?
5	An understanding of abstract concepts (simple) (e.g. time)	Shows an understanding that time passes (e.g. the time of day, waiting, etc.)
5a	An understanding of abstract concepts (complex) (e.g. emotions, morality, etc.)	See play and social development 8
6	An ability to predict in learning (i.e. what happens next)	Is able to work out what might happen next and demonstrate this verbally or through picture (e.g. choice of a range of picture options for a story, etc.)
6a	An ability to predict in people (i.e what they are going to do)	Shows an awareness of what someone is about to do through action (i.e. moves out of the way when someone is moving towards them or is able to demonstrate this verbally through picture e.g. choice of a range of picture options for a story, etc.)
6b	An ability to predict in social settings (i.e what happens next)	See above
6c	An ability to make deductions in learning (i.e. using knowledge to work out an answer or what to do next)	Uses their ability to predict (as above) to work out what they need to do next. (i.e. to problem solve)
6d	An ability to make deductions in social situations (i.e. to work out an answer or what to do next)	See above
6e	An understanding of *implied* meaning or inference (e.g. aren't you cold without a coat?)	As stated. Demonstrates through action or verbally
7	An understanding of informal language or slang expressions (e.g. cut it out, take this chair, etc.)	As stated. Demonstrates through action or verbally
7a	An understanding of jokes, sarcasm and humour	As stated. Demonstrates through action or verbally
7b	An understanding of homonyms, metaphors and similes (e.g. he ran like the wind, the moon sailed across the sky, pins and needles, etc.)	As stated. Demonstrates through action or verbally

Thinking skills and conceptual understanding: Assessment activity and resources

Again, this area is best assessed through observation, practical activity and interaction. Observations made during social and learning based activities are particularly useful for those parts of the assessment which look at understanding of language e.g. items 7. Resources required include a range of play and learning based materials:

- a range of toys and play based activities which encourage problem-solving skills (e.g. puzzles)
- sorting toys and activities
- photos, story sequences and books which provide examples of sequencing, categories and semantic links
- language based materials which specifically address aspects of language such as social problem solving, what happens next, abstract concepts, etc.

ADAPTABILITY

Skill		Example: How does s/he show this?
1	An ability to make choices: needs led (e.g. drink, food)	As stated. Demonstrates through action, symbol or verbally
1a	An ability to make choices: preferences/likes (e.g. choice of toys, videos, etc)	As stated. Demonstrates through action, symbol or verbally
1b	An ability to make choices In social situations (e.g. who to speak to, when to walk away, etc)	As stated. Demonstrates through action, symbol or verbally
1c	An ability to make simple choices in learning (e.g. art materials, books, colours, etc)	As stated. Demonstrates through action, symbol or verbally
1d	An ability to make complex choices in learning (e.g. strategies, options)	As stated. Demonstrates through action, symbol or verbally
2	An ability to cope with 'macro' transitions (e.g. life and big events)	No anxiety over and above what would be expected for the circumstances. Responds to support and information provided
2a	An ability to cope with 'mezzo' transitions (e.g. to different areas/across environments)	No anxiety over and above what would be expected for the circumstances. Responds to support and information provided without difficulty
2b	An ability to cope with 'micro' transitions (e.g. within and between activities)	Moves from activity to activity as requested showing no anxiety or reluctance
3	An acceptance of change to routine or structure	Accepts and responds to change with minimal upset/anxiety
3a	An acceptance of change to rules and procedures	Accepts and responds to change with minimal upset/anxiety
3b	An ability to cope with sudden change, unpredictability and novel activities	Accepts and responds to sudden change with minimal upset/anxiety

continued

Skill		Example: How would s/he show this?
3c	An ability to accept and cope successfully with differing approaches to learning/tasks	Accepts and responds to different approaches (e.g. counting with bricks or with counters, maths in a book or on the computer, etc.) with minimal upset/anxiety
4	An ability to adapt social behaviour to differing situations (e.g. being quiet in the library)	As stated
4a	An understanding of social hierarchy (e.g. the difference between a friend, a teacher and a parent)	Shows this verbally or through picture, written, etc.
4b	An understanding of social hierarchy and an ability to adapt behaviour accordingly	Adapts behaviour according to person and situation
5	Organisation and planning skills: personal (e.g. dressing, self-care, possessions, etc.)	As stated. Able to organise personally with minimal support
5a	Organisation and planning skills in learning (planning, sequencing, carrying out a task)	As stated. Able to organise in task situations with minimal support
5b	Organisation and planning skills in social situations (e.g. planning social outcomes, games, etc.)	As stated. Able to organise socially with minimal support
6	Early problem-solving skills: Trial and error (practical)	As stated. Demonstrates practically and functionally
6a	An ability to identify and apply rules in learning (used to problem solve): practical (e.g. put tops on felt tips, the big bricks go on the bottom, etc.)	As stated. Demonstrates practically and functionally
6b	An ability to identify and apply rules in learning (used to problem solve): starting writing on the left, etc.	As stated. Demonstrates practically and functionally
6c	An ability to identify and apply rules in learning (used to problem solve): Abstract (e.g. always add the units first)	As stated. Demonstrates practically and functionally
6d	Identifying and applying rules in social situations: practical (e.g. if you go in the rain you get wet, ask for help)	As stated. Demonstrates practically and functionally

	Skill	Example: How would s/he show this?
6e	Identifying and applying rules in social situations: simple (e.g. walk on the pavement, follow teacher's instructions, playground games, etc.).	As stated. Demonstrates practically and functionally
6f	Identifying and applying rules in social situations: complex (e.g. don't talk to strangers, offer help to a friend in trouble, etc.)	As stated. Demonstrates practically and functionally
6g	Identifying and applying rules in dealing with everyday situations, practical (e.g. socks before shoes)	As stated. Demonstrates practically and functionally
6h	Identifying and applying rules in dealing with everyday situations (e.g. if you miss a bus wait for the next, etc.)	As stated. Demonstrates practically and functionally
7	An ability to transfer learned skills to new situations (generalisation and flexible use): learning situations	As stated. Demonstrates practically and functionally
7a	An ability to use learned life skills functionally	As stated. Demonstrates practically and functionally
7b	An ability to transfer learned skills to new situations (generalisation and flexible use): across people	As stated. Demonstrates practically and functionally
7c	An ability to transfer learned skills to new situations (generalisation and flexible use): across environments	As stated. Demonstrates practically and functionally

Adaptability: Assessment activity and resources

Again, this area is best assessed through observation, practical activity and interaction. This is an area where information across home and school and other settings is particularly important. Observations made during social and learning based activities are particularly useful for those parts of the assessment which look at organisation and planning such as items 6. Resources required include a range of play and learning based materials:

- a range of toys and play-based activities which encourage problem solving and choice making
- language based materials which specifically address aspects of language such as social problem solving, what happens next, abstract concepts, etc.

The Individual Flexibility Continuum

The Individual Flexibility Continuum can be found in Table 3.6. This is based on the 5P Approach Flexibility Continuum (Table 2.2), adapted specifically to provide a means of recording individual skills and achievements. This continuum provides a visual summative profile for the individual mapping the acquisition of flexibility skills and for plotting progress. It provides a means of identifying continuum 'levels' for each of the three elements of the 5P Approach Flexibility Checklist (Play and Social Development, Thinking and Conceptual Understanding and Adaptability), linking these to an estimated level of independence, and also gives an indication for the type of intervention most suited to the individual's current level of flexibility.

As for the Flexibility Checklist, the Individual Flexibility Continuum is constructed to provide a means of providing a baseline score and also for measuring and recording progress on a termly basis.

Large and small step progress

Progress through large steps is demonstrated in a move through Levels 1–5 for each element of the checklist. The numerical and percentage scoring system used provides a means of measuring small step progress within a level and within each of the three elements. This structure takes account of differences in skill acquisition across the three elements. For example, a pupil may be at Level Two for Play and Social Development and Thinking skills but at Level One for Adaptability.

The numerical scores can also be placed into a database to plot progress over a greater length of time and to allow comparison of degree of progress across individuals or across groups.

Table 3.6 The Individual Flexibility Continuum

Name: DoB: Class:

	LEVEL ONE	LEVEL TWO	LEVEL THREE	LEVEL FOUR	LEVEL FIVE
Recommended teaching approaches and environment associated with level of flexibility	Working with learning style (i.e. creating a safe, structured environment which reduces stress)	Teaching and developing coping strategies within a structured setting	Teaching and developing new skills within a structured setting which offers opportunity for skill development	Flexible and supported approach. Providing opportunities for generalisation of skills taught and learned	Providing opportunities for problem solving and independence (enabling participation)
Current degree of flexibility (descriptor)	Rigid/inflexible in behaviour and learning (narrow focus and interests)	Use of strategies (taught or self-developed) to *cope* successfully with change, choice or challenge	Developing new skills in flexibility	Using newly acquired skills in different situations with prompt	Acquired independence in thought – no/ minimal prompts

Monitoring		B	T1	T2	T3	B	T1	T2	T3	B	T1	T2	T3	B	T1	T2	T3	B	T1	T2	T3
Play and social development	/205																				
	%																				
Thinking skills and conceptual understanding	/120																				
	%																				
Adaptability	/155																				
	%																				

Current level of independence	Fully supported/ passive	Partially supported/ partial independence – using coping strategies	Partially supported/ partial independence – developing new skills	Independent – with minimal external support or prompt	Fully independent – may use self-prompt strategies

Baseline	Term One	Term Two	Term Three

Date completed:

Completed by:

How to use this Continuum: Record the assessed Level of Flexibility (from the Flexibility Checklist) for each element in the appropriate column. Record total score for each heading to identify progress within a Level. Record in numerical and in percentage form. Please provide date of assessment to provide a record of progress and achievement.

Copyright © Linda Miller 2013

The SP Approach

Table 3.7 The Individual Flexibility Continuum Example

Name: DoB: Class:

		LEVEL ONE				LEVEL TWO				LEVEL THREE				LEVEL FOUR				LEVEL FIVE			
Recommended teaching approaches and environment associated with level of flexibility		Working with learning style (i.e. creating a safe, structured environment which reduces stress)				Teaching and developing coping strategies within a structured setting				Teaching and developing new skills within a structured setting which offers opportunity for skill development				Flexible and supported approach. Providing opportunities for generalisation of skills taught and learned				Providing opportunities for problem solving and independence (enabling participation)			
Current degree of flexibility (descriptor)		Rigid/inflexible in behaviour and learning (narrow focus and interests)				Use of strategies (taught or self-developed) to cope successfully with change, choice or challenge				Developing new skills in flexibility				Using newly acquired skills in different situations with prompt				Acquired independence in thought – no/ minimal prompts			
Monitoring		B	T1	T2	T3	B	T1	T2	T3	B	T1	T2	T3	B	T1	T2	T3	B	T1	T2	T3
Play and social development	/205	63	75					84	101												
	%	30	35					41	49												
Thinking skills and conceptual understanding	/120					45	60					65	78								
	%					37	50					54	65								
Adaptability	/155	40					60	80					92								
	%	26					39	52					59								
Current level of independence		Fully supported/ passive				Partially supported/ partial independence – using coping strategies				Partially supported/ partial independence – developing new skills				Independent – with minimal external support or prompt				Fully independent – may use self-prompt strategies			

	Baseline	Term One	Term Two	Term Three
Date completed:	September 2012	December 2012	March 2012	July 2012
Completed by:	LM	LM	LM	LM

How to use this Continuum: Record the assessed Level of Flexibility (from the Flexibility Checklist) for each element in the appropriate column. Record total score for each heading to identify progress within a Level. Record in numerical and in percentage form. Please provide date of assessment to provide a record of progress and achievement.

Completing the Individual Flexibility Continuum

The Individual Flexibility Continuum is constructed to provide a means of providing a baseline score (B on the profile) and also for measuring and recording progress on a termly basis (T1, T2 and T3). Progress through larger steps is demonstrated in a move through Levels 1–5 (the vertical columns). The numerical and percentage scoring system used provides a means of measuring small step progress within a level and within each of the three elements.

Total numerical scores obtained from the checklist for each element (i.e. Play and Social Development, Thinking and Conceptual Understanding and Adaptability) are mapped on the Individual Flexibility Continuum. Baseline or T1, T2 or T3 scores obtained are placed within the sub-column along with a percentage score under the appropriate Level column (Levels for the total scores can be taken from the key at the end of each section). Total numerical scores obtained from the checklist for each element are mapped on the Individual Flexibility Continuum placed under the appropriate Level column and then within the Baseline or T1, T2 or T3 sub-column along with a percentage score (calculated separately using the formula: raw score ÷ total score × 100). Use of the percentage score allows the mapping of progress in smaller steps than a movement from one level to another. An example of a completed continuum can be found in Table 3.7. For quick reference assessors can use different coloured pens or shading for each different timescale.

Percentages can also be placed in graph form to provide a graphic picture of clear small step progression over time. An example can be found in Table 3.8.

Table 3.8 Percentage Graph

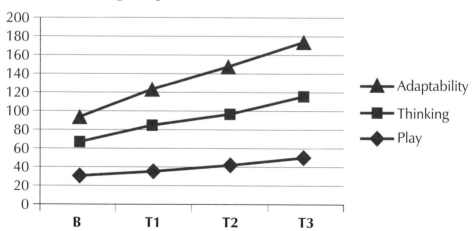

65

The Flexibility Target Sheet

This can be found in Table 3.9. The Flexibility Target Sheet is used in conjunction with the individual's IEP or personalised learning plan and provides a format for recording current levels of ability within each of the three Flexibility Checklist elements, next steps or targets, expected outcomes and strategies and resources needed.

Identifying priorities and setting targets

The 5P Approach Flexibility Assessment contains a number of statements all representing flexibility skills. Although the completed assessment provides a comprehensive overview of the individual's flexibility skills and level of development, it would not be practical to identify targets for every skill identified. Taking one skill for each of the three elements (i.e. Play and Social Development, Thinking and Conceptual Understanding and Adaptability) priorities for intervention are identified on the following basis:

- those areas which present a major challenge in terms of barriers to learning, well-being or behaviour

- those which are easiest to address and plan for.

The Flexibility Target Sheet (Table 3.9) provides a format for recording flexibility targets and strategies or alternatively these targets and strategies may be placed within an individual's IEP or personalised learning plan. You can find ideas for strategies and resources to address some of the skill areas within Chapter 4 and Chapter 5.

Table 3.9 The Flexibility Target Sheet

Name:

Date:

Flexibility Element, Item and Skill	Current level of flexibility and item score	Current approach and teaching strategies used	Developing flexibility: next steps (or new skill?)	Target (outcome)	Strategies (including prompts)	Review date	Achieved? (or improved score?)
Play and social development Item and Skill							
Thinking skills and conceptual understanding Item and Skill							
Adaptability Item and Skill							

Chapter 4

USING THE 5P APPROACH FLEXIBILITY ASSESSMENT IN INTERVENTION PLANNING

You have used the 5P Approach Flexibility Assessment and have a picture of the individual's skills and identified areas for development. Now it is time to begin planning for intervention. Where do you start?

As described in Chapter 3, the 5P Approach Flexibility Assessment can be used to create a baseline profile. The information it provides however is not just to identify new targets and monitor progress. It also gives a picture of current strengths and points us to what type of environment and strategies will work with the individual's current level of flexibility. This is the first step in creating a GREEN Zone.

For example, if we have a child who scores at Level One for all three elements of the continuum, we would assume this child to be fairly rigid and inflexible in his or her thinking. Looking at the corresponding environment and teaching strategies for Level One on the Flexibility Continuum (as in Table 2.2), this child would need a highly structured and supported environment to reduce any stress (and any consequent behaviour issues) and to create an environment in which the child can learn, move forward and make progress. However, this is only a *general* rule of thumb. In order to create a personalised flexibility plan there is a need to look at the individual's profile in more detail and use this to inform our planning.

What else do you need to know before starting? Although the 5P Approach Flexibility Assessment will provide information about an individual's flexibility skills, it does not provide a *whole* picture. If we want to personalise a plan we will also need to look at the individual's interests, likes and dislikes, other strengths and weaknesses, how they like to learn, how they best communicate and so forth. The 5P Approach Profile, introduced in *Practical Behaviour Management Solutions for Children and Teens with Autism – The 5P Approach*, provides a quick reference format for collecting all this information. The 5P Approach Profile is reproduced in Figure 4.1.

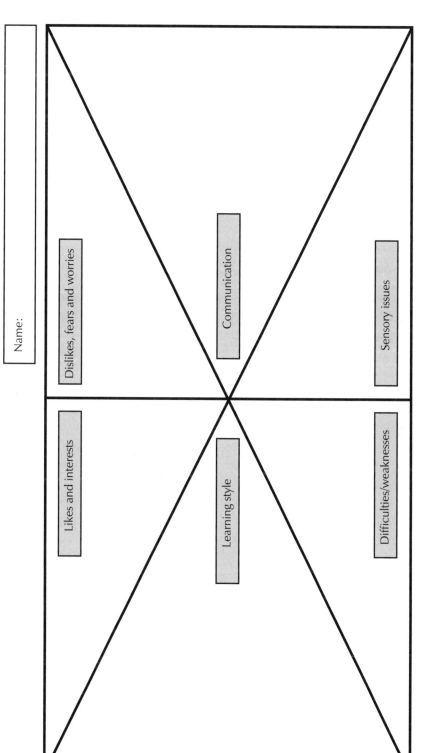

Name:

Dislikes, fears and worries

Communication

Sensory issues

Likes and interests

Learning style

Difficulties/weaknesses

Figure 4.1: The 5P Approach Profile

Creating a personalised flexibility intervention plan

As described in Chapter 2, the 5P Approach to Flexibility, as with the 5P Approach to behaviour intervention, places a focus on developing skills and creating foundations (the GREEN Zone) which prevent behaviour issues from arising and support the development of flexibility skills and independence. Using the principles and philosophy of the 5P Approach, the 5P Approach to Flexibility uses the distinct traffic light colours to outline a flexibility intervention framework, summarised within the four 5P Approach Flexibility Strands:

1. The general intervention approach – creating the GREEN Zone

2. Developing flexibility skills (GREEN)

3. Providing opportunities to develop flexibility (GREEN)

4. Teaching coping or self-management strategies (AMBER).

These four strands (plus five if there is a RED behaviour issue!) therefore form the basis of the flexibility intervention plan. The 5P Approach Flexibility Strands Planner (Figure 4.2) provides a visual pro-forma for recording the plan. This can be completed and added to any IEP or preventative behaviour intervention plan or, alternatively, the information from the planner can be incorporated into any existing plans.

In line with the 5P Approach preventative philosophy, this Flexibility Strands Planner is not set into place only when an issue arises but rather forms the basis of the overall (preventative) plan for supporting that individual from the word go. That is, *not* what we do when something goes wrong *but* what we do to meet the individual's needs and prevent things from going wrong.

Again, in line with the 5P Approach philosophy of learning from experience and continuing to build GREEN, as new skills develop and new issues arise (and new strategies to support them) these are added to the plan and the GREEN Zone expands.

Having this set out in a clear plan means that this can be shared with all those working with the individual (and of course the individual themselves) to ensure consistency and continuity of approach whatever the environment or situation.

Name: Date:

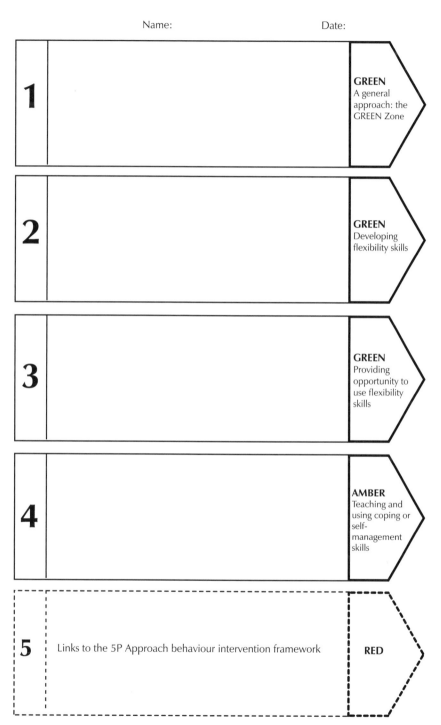

1   GREEN
A general
approach: the
GREEN Zone

2   GREEN
Developing
flexibility skills

3   GREEN
Providing
opportunity to
use flexibility
skills

4   AMBER
Teaching and
using coping or
self-
management
skills

5   Links to the 5P Approach behaviour intervention framework   RED

Figure 4.2: The 5P Approach Flexibility Strands Planner

How to fill out the Flexibility Strands Planner

Each strand of the planner is completed using information from the 5P Approach Flexibility Assessment, the 5P Profile and knowledge about the individual. We begin by asking (and answering) the following questions:

1. What is the overall level of flexibility for each element?

- What does this indicate in terms of the *general* approach to be adopted?

Using the 5P Approach Flexibility Continuum Strategy Guidance (Table 4.1) and knowledge about current successful strategies in use, this information is placed in Strand One (general approaches) to begin to outline the GREEN zone for that individual.

Table 4.1 The Flexibility Continuum – Strategy Guidance

	LEVEL ONE	LEVEL TWO	LEVEL THREE	LEVEL FOUR	LEVEL FIVE
Teaching Approaches and Environment Guidance	Working with the learning style Creating a safe, structured environment for the reduction of stress A highly structured and visually supported environment (pictures or symbols). Clear, and well organised with little change Use of approaches such as TEACCH. Use of short visual timetables for direction Activities have clear beginning and end Minimal change and transition Rule based and structured approach to teaching and learning	Teaching and developing coping strategies: A structured approach with some challenge and change and taught opportunity to use coping strategies Developing from Level One Increased *prompted* use of schedules and timetables (towards independence) Opportunities for supported transition and change Structured timetable and activities including some structured and taught elements of choice and surprise	Teaching and developing new skills: A structured approach with some challenge and change and opportunity to use newly developing skills Developing from Level Two Independent use of timetables and transition support Increased presentation of problem-solving opportunities, choice, change and creativity Slow decrease in use of prompts and increase in use of newly developing skills	Providing opportunities for generalisation of skills taught and learned: A less structured and predictable approach Developing from Levels One to Three Moving towards group timetable/diary system rather than individual Less structured timetable with increased opportunities for more complex social and learning, problem solving and creativity Increased opportunities for choice Independent use of visual support as needed Increased opportunity for the functional use and generalisation of newly acquired skills	Providing opportunities for problem solving and independence: Minimal structure, maximum opportunity for independent thinking and behaviour Developing from Levels One to Four Less specialised and structured timetable and activities Minimum use of prompts and support (as needed) Increased independence and independent use of acquired skills and self-management strategies

Then, taking each element at a time ask:

2. What skills have been achieved or are almost there (scores of 4 and 5)?

These are the areas where the individual should be given opportunity to use and generalise his or her skills. What opportunities should the individual have? Do these require support or resources? This information is added to Strand Three (providing opportunity).

3. Which skills are not yet present (score 1)?

- Are these *priorities* for new skill teaching? (If so set as a target – see below.)
- What strategies can be put into place to support the child and reduce any stress caused by a lack of flexibility skills until new skills develop?

This information is added to the more general information in Strand One (general approaches) to provide some specific personal guidance for areas of particular difficulty.

4. Which skills are emerging (scores of 2 and 3)?

- What strategies or support is required to help these skills to establish?

This information is added to Strand Two (developing skills). Strand Two should also contain any information about specific targets (new skills) which may have been identified and how these will be addressed. This section can cross reference to the Flexibility Target Sheet or the individual's IEP.

5. What coping or managing strategies can be put into place?

- How will the individual use these?
- Does this require the child to learn a new skill and how will we teach or support it?
- What resources are needed?

This is where generally the individual would need to use a coping or managing strategy either as a long-term strategy to overcome any difficulties presented or as a short-term strategy while skills develop. These are recorded in Strand Four (coping or self-managing).

Developing independence – don't be complacent!

As we have seen, the development and use of flexibility skills is a key feature of developing independence in thought, in learning and in behaviour. Our aim then should be always to support the individual to move further along the Flexibility Continuum and further towards independence.

Once we have created a flexibility intervention plan and a GREEN Zone, it doesn't stop there! When first creating the intervention plan and setting out the GREEN Zone strategies, the philosophy is to support the individual by addressing their level of flexibility with an approach which matches that level. For example we support rigid behaviour with a rigid or structured approach to create a stable and supportive base upon which to progress. The focus should always be on moving forward but at a speed and in a manner which develops the individual without stress or anxiety. For example we may support a child who has difficulty with change by giving him a particular chair to sit on when he comes into a group activity. This has created a firm base which works with his current rigid style. It reduces stress, becomes a pattern of behaviour and the child successfully sits as part of the group. However if we leave it there we may have solved one flexibility problem but have created another (he will now only sit on that chair in that place!). Gradually then we build in the next flexibility steps. For example we may stick to the same chair but move the position, we may label the chair and move the label to other chairs, then make the label smaller and smaller until it isn't needed. The speed of change and type of strategy should be decided upon according to the individual, but the focus should always be on next flexibility steps rather than creating and sticking to another rigid pattern.

This also means making sure that when we decide upon a strategy to support an individual we also look at how they might be able to use this independently and, if this isn't possible straight away, how we can support them to get to that stage.

It also means making sure that the individual has the opportunity to use any new skills taught or developed functionally, that is put into practical use across a range of settings or people. Those with flexibility issues frequently have problems with generalising skills or knowledge learned into other situations or settings. There is no guarantee that if she or he is taught a skill in one place (e.g. in the classroom) a child will automatically be able to use this in another setting (e.g. in the playground or home). Any plan therefore should build in how functional use and generalisation of skills can be supported.

This is particularly important in the way we put coping or management strategies into place. In the first instance, there may be a need to be fairly directive in approach in order to establish the pattern of behaviour and demonstrate to the individual that this is a strategy that will be useful. However, once the pattern of behaviour is established there is a need to gradually reduce the prompts and support until the individual can use the strategy independently. For example, we may support a child who has difficulties with transitions by using a match back system: that is, a child will take the symbol depicting the next place to go (e.g. the library) from a visual timetable and take it with him to the library 'posting' it (into a folder) or sticking it to the door (Velcro strip) which has the same symbol. The first step may be to physically take the child to the timetable, remove the symbol for him, and support him to hold it all the way to the library and post it at the door. This gradually changes until the child can manage the whole process independently moving on to a stage where the child can look at the timetable and make the room change without the need to take a symbol with him.

There are some practical examples of strategies like this in Chapter 5.

Developing skills – target setting

Chapter 3 outlines the 5P Approach Flexibility Assessment and introduces the Flexibility Target Sheet (Table 3.9). In addition to providing a framework for the recording of targets, strategies and outcomes for skills within each of the three Flexibility Elements (Play and Social Development, Thinking and Conceptual Understanding and Adaptability) the format of the target sheet encourages the gradual development of flexibility skills as outlined above. Instead of simply identifying a target from assessment and strategies and proposed outcome as in most IEPs, the Flexibility Target Sheet outlines a flexibility development process.

The headings of the Flexibility Target Sheet are set out in Table 4.2.

Table 4.2 Flexibility Target Sheet Headings

Flexibility Element, Item and Skill	Current level of flexibility and item score	Current approach and teaching strategies used	Developing flexibility: next steps (or new skill)	Target (outcome)	Strategies (including prompts)	Review date	Achieved? (or improved score?)

The first step is to prioritise skills for development and the identified Flexibility Element, Item and Skill taken from the Flexibility Checklist is then recorded in the first column. In the second and third column, the corresponding current level of flexibility and individual item score is recorded along with current approaches used for that item.

In the fourth column the next step or new skill is recorded. This next step could be using the flexibility skill with the reduction or absence of prompts (i.e. independently), using the skill functionally, or moving on to the next skill to be achieved. The proposed outcome (target) is recorded in the next column and then new strategies. An example of a completed Flexibility Target Sheet can be found in Table 4.3.

Table 4.3 The Flexibility Target Sheet Example

Name: Date:

Flexibility Element, Item and Skill	Current level of flexibility and item score	Current approach and teaching strategies used	Developing flexibility: next steps (or new skill?)	Target (outcome)	Strategies (including prompts)	Review date	Achieved? (or improved score?)
Play and social development **Item and skill:** 1b exploratory play	Level One 2 (emerging)	A small range (3–4) of toys within her interests (using motivator list) one at a time. X encouraged to spend time (1 minute +) with each toy in succession supported by visual (photo) prompt. Exploration encouraged by modelling and prompt (hand over hand)	Move to Score 3–4 developing and using new skills	To independently explore the 4 toys visually and physically (i.e. turning, looking, pressing buttons, etc.) moving from one toy to another without visual prompt	Present toys all at once. Use photo to direct and encourage change of toy if needed. Continue to model and prompt exploratory skills but wait before prompting. Use minimal prompt and reduce asap		
Thinking skills and conceptual understanding **Item and skill:** 4 understanding categories	Level One 1 (not present)	Three different balls (size and colour) and 3 different cups (size, shape and colour). Table top setting moving to carpet play setting. One ball and one cup placed on separate identical trays, sorting modelled and using hand over hand prompts	Move to Score 2–3 emerging and developing skill	To independently sort 3 different items (balls, cups and cars) into groups with minimal prompting, in formal activity and tidying toys	As previous but removing band over band prompt, use gesture to prompt if needed. Move to functional toy tidying activity		
Adaptability **Item and skill:** 3c Coping with sudden change	Level One 2 (emerging)	Use of structured visual timetable and routine. Use of 'this–then' card to remind of what is next if sudden unplanned change. Close support to reduce stress if needed	Move to 4 using new skills	To respond to 'surprise' card on timetable showing no signs of stress. (Hold surprise card and new activity/ change card during surprise item and follow direction as required)	Introduction of 'surprise' card on timetable beginning with favoured activity as surprise. X to remove surprise card and next activity to a this–then board to hold while activity happens. Physical and band over hands prompts reduced asap		

Links to behaviour management and behaviour intervention plans

The 5P Approach to Flexibility links with behaviour management and planning in three ways: to contribute to the overall preventative approach or GREEN Zone, as part of the process of working out what is happening and why (Problem analysis and Problem solving), and finally in the 5P Planning process.

The GREEN Zone

As described in Chapter 2, the 5P Approach to behaviour intervention, like the 5P Approach to Flexibility, places a strong emphasis on prevention and the creation of a GREEN Zone. Any 5P Approach behaviour intervention plan would include GREEN strategies and approaches, and the teaching of new skills and coping or self-managing. Information gained through the 5P Flexibility Assessment and planning process is a major contributor to this.

Behaviour management

When worrying behaviour issues (RED behaviours) arise, whether these be signs of anxiety and distress, anger or non-engagement, this is where the 5P Approach to behaviour intervention (as described in *Practical Behaviour Management Solutions for Children and Teens with Autism – The 5P Approach*) comes in, working alongside the 5P Approach to Flexibility.

Rather than simply reacting to a RED behaviour and 'managing' it, the 5P Approach follows a process of problem analysis and problem solving to identify the *function* of the behaviour causing concern. In the 5P Approach, behaviour management becomes behaviour intervention, that is: a broader approach which involves constructing a plan designed to prevent (GREEN) or pre-empt (AMBER) behaviour issues from arising so that the need for management of challenging behaviour (RED) is at a minimum.

The very first step in the 5P process (the first 'P') is Profile, to know that individual well. The qualitative information gathered from the 5P Approach Flexibility Assessment adds to that of the 5P Profile and gives a useful insight into whether (and what) flexibility issues may be underlying the behaviour issues. This then can be used as part of the problem-solving process. For example: an individual shows signs of distress when a supply teacher takes the class and we are aware from flexibility assessment that coping with change is an issue. Knowledge about what type of strategies will be useful (from the 5P Flexibility Assessment) for this individual also contributes to the planning phase.

Where RED issues occur, a 5P Approach Intervention Hierarchy (Table 2.1) is constructed which comprises identification of GREEN, AMBER and RED behaviours and corresponding strategies. In many cases flexibility issues are an underlying or contributing factor to behaviour issues and the GREEN strategies and new skills to be developed and AMBER coping or management strategies are the same as those found within the Flexibility Strands Planner.

Behaviour intervention plans

When challenging behaviour issues occur, depending on the emphasis required for the individual concerned or professionals working with them, the link between the 5P Approach and the 5P Approach to Flexibility can be represented in two ways.

1. Creating a Flexibility Intervention Plan which comprises:

- The Flexibility Assessment Summary

- The Flexibility Strands Planner

- The Flexibility Target Sheet

- The 5P Approach Intervention Hierarchy (for specific RED behaviours only with a view to the GREEN and AMBER strategies being included within the Flexibility Strands Planner once the behaviour issues have reduced).

2. Creating a 5P Approach positive intervention plan which comprises:

- The 5P Profile

- An outline of the GREEN Zone (including the Flexibility Strands Planner)

- The 5P Approach Planning Summary and associated records

- The 5P Approach Intervention Hierarchy.

The 5P Approach to Flexibility therefore can be applied as a distinct stand-alone approach or used as part of the 5P Approach to behaviour intervention. Where flexibility issues are linked with a significant degree of challenging behaviour however, the 5P Approach to behaviour intervention should be the main tool using the 5P Approach to Flexibility materials to provide additional information.

Staying GREEN – building good foundations to support the development of flexibility

As described in the first chapters of this book, the 5P Approach to Flexibility, its philosophy and framework and the Flexibility Assessment can be used with individuals to create a specific and personalised intervention plan, assess key flexibility skills and to monitor progress. However the approach can also be used with groups (classes, residential units, etc.) and with whole organisations as part of developing a wider flexibility policy or flexibility curriculum.

The four Flexibility Strands – having a general intervention approach (creating the GREEN Zone), developing flexibility skills, providing opportunities to develop flexibility and teaching coping or management strategies – can all be expanded for group and organisational use to create flexibility-friendly environments which serve to break down the barriers caused by poor flexibility, that is, by reducing stress caused by flexibility issues and supporting the development of independence in thought, learning and behaviour. This is explored further in Chapter 7.

Chapter 5

STAYING GREEN AND DEVELOPING FLEXIBILITY

Ideas and resources
(with contributions from Louise Miller)

This chapter looks specifically at three areas which often present particular challenges for those with poor flexibility: transitions, problem solving and adaptability. More general flexibility ideas and resources can be found in Chapter 7.

Transitions

What do we mean by transition? Transition is about change. For the purposes of this chapter, a transition is defined as any change or movement from one thing to another whether that be a place, a person, an activity or an event.

Transitions may be big life changes or events (known as macro transitions), smaller, less intensive (mezzo) changes or very small micro changes which to those with good flexibility skills don't seem to be changes at all.

Macro (large) transitions include those life changing events such as a change of school, job or house; moving from one education phase to another, such as from nursery into school, school to college and so forth. This category also includes significant life events such as having a new sibling, a family breakdown or family death, family and school holidays and puberty.

Mezzo (medium) transitions are those which have less of an impact but still represent change. These include the daily move from home to school and vice versa; visits within the community such as to the shops, swimming pool, library; having a change of teacher or carer; the appearance of visitors and sudden or unexpected surprises (good or bad).

Micro or very small transitions are those such as a change of timetable, moving from one room to another or a change in the environment such as noise, heat (this could also involve sensory processing issues), weather, others' emotions and moods. This can also include changing between and within activities.

So why are transitions so difficult for those with poor flexibility? Managing transitions, even the smallest ones, requires a degree of adaptability and flexibility. It requires skills such as being able to predict or anticipate what will happen next, to think back (and forwards) and make connections with previous experiences (What will happen? What happened last time?). It requires the ability to plan and organise, to problem solve and make choices and to understand the passage of time (How long will this be? When will this end? When is 'soon'?). It also involves social understanding (taking social cues and reading people and situations) and it requires a degree of self-knowledge and self-reflection (What am I expected to do? How will I feel? How will I know if I am doing the right thing?).

If we look back at the description of flexibility in Chapter 1, we can see that all these skills, essential for the successful management of transition, are skills related to flexibility of thought and are therefore frequently areas of difficulty for those with poor flexibility. If you have poor flexibility, a tendency to be rigid or ritualistic in your behaviour and approach (I must do this to the end and in this way!), have a narrow focus and restricted interests (I am not interested and don't want to change) and difficulty with planning, organising and sequencing (thinking, planning and doing) it is no wonder that change and transition will be difficult for you or that this could then lead to anxiety or fear and consequently to behaviour difficulty.

However, even though we may assume that transition may cause fear, anxiety and behaviour responses, whenever we are looking at how to support the individual, there is still a need to dig deep and work out why the problem occurs (i.e. the function of the behaviour) before we can successfully work out a solution. This is where the 5P Approach problem-solving framework can be useful.

The ability to cope with change and transition is therefore linked closely to flexible thinking and, as such, managing transitions should be seen as part of flexibility skills training within a flexibility curriculum and should be placed firmly on the Flexibility Continuum (see below).

So what do we do and how can we help?

Managing transitions and developing skills

As can been seen above, understanding and coping with transitions is a key area of difficulty linked to flexibility of thought and, as such, means that individuals who have problems with transitions (of any sort) require some specific support and intervention. Developing the skills needed to make successful transitions requires intervention which provides the four 5P Flexibility Strands (Figure 2.1):

1. A general intervention approach (Creating the GREEN Zone) which works with the individual's learning style, creating a safe environment which reduces stress and from which the individual can move forward.

2. Developing transition (flexibility) skills. Supporting the individual to develop the skills needed to cope successfully with transition and to move further towards independence. (GREEN)

3. Providing opportunities to use and generalise transition skills, i.e. to experience transitions in a wide variety of ways (i.e. micro, mezzo, and macro) and across differing environments and activities. (GREEN)

4. Teaching coping and self-management strategies. Supporting the individual to use strategies which act as coping or self-management strategies while new skills develop. (AMBER)

As with other flexibility skill development, the four Flexibility Strands work together to provide a best practice model for transition management and skill development.

Again using the distinctive traffic light colours, GREEN represents the strategies and approaches which form the foundations upon which to develop transition skills within a safe and supportive environment.

AMBER represents the coping or self-management strategies as described in the previous chapter.

In addition, AMBER includes additional 'teacher' strategies used to pre-empt or prevent transitions from breaking down. If an individual begins to show signs of transition breakdown (e.g. anxiety and/or behaviour issues – sometimes known as bubbling behaviour) these AMBER strategies are used to provide additional support, to re-focus and reassure the individual and move them back to GREEN.

Additional strategies used at AMBER would be those such as reminding the individual what is coming next using a 'this–then' card, providing a transition object, giving time and space and so on. Further examples of strategies that can be used to support transitions both at GREEN and AMBER can be found later in this chapter.

RED (a place to avoid!) represents transition breakdown of a serious nature where the individual now requires specific management and a clear signal that behaviour has reached a RED level (RED strategies). Using the 5P Approach Intervention Hierarchy, the focus is then on moving back to GREEN as quickly as possible. RED management strategies are therefore followed by strategies which encourage the individual to calm. When the individual is once again receptive to direction (at AMBER), strategies are used to refocus, re-present the request to transition with support and then finally move back to GREEN.

The 5P Approach philosophy is that lessons should be learned if a student reaches AMBER and RED before or during a transition. This means reviewing and analysing the situation that occurred, thinking about why there were problems and reviewing the strategies which should be in use to prevent transition breakdown

(GREEN). Once established and successful in reducing stress and ensuring a smooth transition, these can then become part of the everyday approach to this particular transition (and added to the GREEN Zone).

Transition and the Flexibility Continuum

Just as developing flexibility of thought can be seen as part of a continuum of developing skills which is linked to teaching approaches and to the level of independence, managing transitions can equally be seen as a process along a continuum. Placing the development of transition skills within a continuum in this way ensures that we maximise opportunity for the development of independence and that the strategies used change as transition (flexibility) skills emerge and establish.

As with the Flexibility Continuum set out in Chapter 2 (Table 2.2), the approaches and strategies used by the individual or supporting adult relate directly to the skill level of the individual, e.g. Level 1 on the continuum would mean that an individual is very rigid and generally has extreme difficulty with transitions. This would mean that they require the highest level of structure and maximum strategies and support for transitions. Table 5.1 shows how managing transitions sits within the Flexibility Continuum.

We can see from the descriptions in this chapter that transitions can vary considerably in nature. Different transitions may require different types and levels of flexibility skill and an individual may have acquired the skills needed to manage some transitions and not others. Therefore these continuum levels (and thus type and degree of support needed) can equally apply to different *activities and situations*. For example, transition to a new activity or environment which has been identified as a *probable* cause of stress (an AMBER warning!) should initially be placed at Level 1 and planned with maximum support and structure until the activity becomes more familiar, the individual develops the knowledge and skills needed to successfully manage the transition and the level of support can be reduced (i.e. the individual moves up the continuum).

Table 5.1 The 5P Approach Flexibility Continuum – Transitions

	LEVEL ONE	LEVEL TWO	LEVEL THREE	LEVEL FOUR	LEVEL FIVE
Teaching Approaches and Environment for TRANSITIONS	Working with the learning style. Creating a safe, structured environment. Highly structured approach with **maximum** signal and support (e.g. very clear end and beginning structured use of changeover time, visual, physical and verbal prompts, schedules)	Teaching and developing coping strategies	Teaching and developing new skills	Providing opportunities for generalisation of skills taught and learned	Providing opportunities for problem solving and independence. Minimum prompt and support (e.g. verbal reminder schedules) (where needed). Using environmental cues
		Decrease level of prompting **Move from physical/artificial and concrete prompts to environmental cues** →			
Degree of Flexibility	Rigid/inflexible in behaviour and learning (Narrow focus and interests)	Use of strategies (taught or self developed) to cope successfully with change, choice or challenge	Developing new skills in flexibility (e.g. tolerance, making choices and decisions, problem solving, understanding abstract concepts, etc.)	Using newly acquired skills in different situations with prompt (e.g. generalisation, adaptability, problem solving). Demonstrated in learning and behaviour	Acquired independence in thought. No or minimal prompts needed. Demonstrated in learning and behaviour
Level of Independence	Fully supported and mainly passive in interaction. Low level of independence	Partially supported/ partial independence – using coping strategies	Partially supported/ partial independence – developing new skills	Independent – with minimal external support or prompt	Fully independent – may use self-prompt strategies

Practical strategies for managing transitions

This section provides some practical strategies and ideas for supporting transitions, first by providing some general strategies and guidance and second by giving some situation specific ideas.

General strategies (GREEN)

GREEN strategies are those put into place to prevent or pre-empt issues from arising. If we know an individual's level of flexibility and the type of things that cause stress, we can pre-empt by identifying transitions which may cause a problem and putting in strategies to support and prevent any problems from occurring. For example, potential AMBER (bubbly) situations are those such as moving from one place to another (room to room or from table to carpet, etc.), changing from one activity to another, starting an activity, finishing off an activity, etc. Often, but not always, this is about making sure you have communicated (and the individual understands) what the transition is and the reason for it clearly and effectively.

For moving from one place to another this means communicating:

- *What* is happening (this can be verbal, written or through use of pictures, objects, etc.)

- *When* things are happening (using a 'this–then' card, schedules or calendars, diaries, timetables, clocks and timers, etc.)

- *How long* they will be (using clocks, timers, 'pingers', songs, calendars, etc.)

- *Where* things will happen (this can be verbal, written or through use of pictures, photos, etc.)

- *Who* will be there (this can be verbal, written or using lists of names, name cards, photos, etc.)

- *How* will you get there? (this can be verbal, written or through use of pictures, objects, etc.)

- *What* will happen next? (next activity, reward, etc., verbal or through pictures or schedule).

For more able individuals with good language skills, it may seem sufficient to let them know all of this verbally. However, even if you know and understand the words themselves, if you have flexibility problems (and therefore poor executive function and poor central coherence), you may not be able to retain and use the information in the way you need to or when you need to (When is soon? or How long is 20 minutes? Which order do things happen in?). Anxiety in these circumstances often presents as repetitive questioning, an attempt to make sense of things and be clear. Therefore, even with those individuals who may present as if they have the skills they need to take all this in, it is best to provide some of the visual support as set out above. This would include, for those who are more able, reminding and supporting the individual to write things down themselves which will provide a self-management strategy and increase independence.

For transitions within tasks and activities rather than movement, this means communicating:

- *What* they have to do – including what they will need (through demonstration, written list, symbols, photos or diagram, model, etc.)

- *How much* they have to do – and how they know they have finished (using a written or pictorial task list or mini-schedule)

- *What* they do at the end (using a 'this–then' card, a written or visual timetable)

- *What* will come next (activity? reward? using a 'this–then' card, a written or visual timetable, photo, object).

As with the previous list, it is important not to make assumptions that because an individual has the ability to understand the information and do what is required of them, they also have the planning, organisation and sequencing (executive function) skills they need to remember and follow through all the necessary steps and actions without some additional support. However able an individual is considered to be, this is often an area of difficulty and one which causes stress.

Some examples of visual materials (mini-schedules) used to support transitions in this way are found in Figures 5.1–5.3.

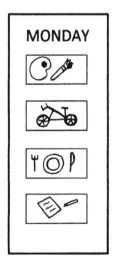 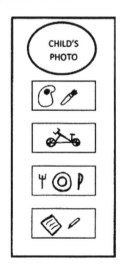 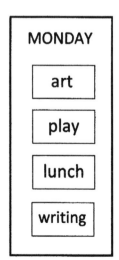

Figure 5.1: A Symbol Mini-Schedule   *Figure 5.2: A Symbol Mini-Schedule with Child's Photo*   *Figure 5.3: A Written Mini-Schedule*

Planning activities

Planned activities should have a clear start, middle and end and there should be a clear signal for starting and ending and changing in and between sessions. For example, demonstrate start or finish by using music or song, lowering lights, using countdowns (verbal, fingers or number line) or timers.

Lessons and activities for more able individuals should similarly be divided into defined steps or stages (recorded on a white board or a list, etc.) and the end and beginning of each stage signalled.

As well as letting the individual know about what activity is next, visual lists can be used to depict what materials or resources are needed for a task and what order they are used in. For example, a painting activity: get your apron, then get paper, then get paint brush and then paint. As well as supporting the micro transitions between steps of the task, this also supports problem solving and 'think, plan and do' and of course encourages independence rather than reliance on a series of prompts. A visual schedule for this is shown in Figure 5.4.

Figure 5.4: Painting Activity Schedule

Moving from one place to another

GREEN strategies (put in place to prevent) to support transitioning from one place to another are those such as:

- All types of visual schedule (from objects, first–then, mini and full schedules). More able students can have a written timetable or diary. Example of schedules and 'first–then' cards can be found in Figure 5.5. Specific travelling schedules which set out the process of a regular transition (for example a trip to the shop) are particularly useful and can be prepared in advance alongside a social story which sets out what happens, when and why and what happens afterwards. Again, these can be presented in a way that is most suitable for the individual's level of ability and understanding.

- Use of a portable white board or note pad to show the next two activities (the individual could write or draw it themselves).

- Use of a reward schedule such as 'I am working for…' (see Figure 5.6) to reinforce the transition to the next activity (a token is given at the end of each activity). For more able individuals, this can be presented as a task list or tick list with a reward or rewarding activity at the end. Further examples of different reward strategies can be found in *Practical Behaviour Management Solutions for Children and Teens with Autism – The 5P Approach*.

- 'Posting' schedule cards at the next place. This is known as using match backs or baseboards. The principle as described earlier is to take a picture or written label from the schedule or timetable and carry it to the next area or place, posting it in a folder or sticking it to a matching picture or label found at the next place. A visual example of this can be found in Figure 5.7.

- Use of transition objects (e.g. carrying a paint brush to art area, PE bag to gym, etc.)

- Lines or footsteps to follow. More able students can have a map of the area or building showing any distinctive markers e.g. staff room, water cooler, etc.

- Counting steps or counting markers to the next place.

- Using rest stops (markers or specific places to stop at and calm for a while or stopping off at an activity on the way (timed)).

- Using sensory activities such as music players, stress reduction toys (e.g. Koosh ball), weighted jackets (on occupational therapy advice), etc. As well as reducing sensory based stress they also act as distractors.

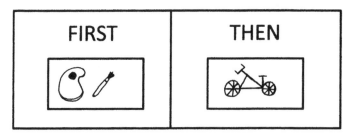

Figure 5.5: First, Then

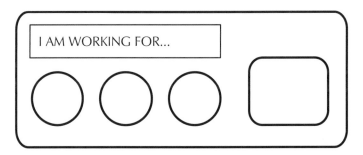

Figure 5.6: I am Working for...

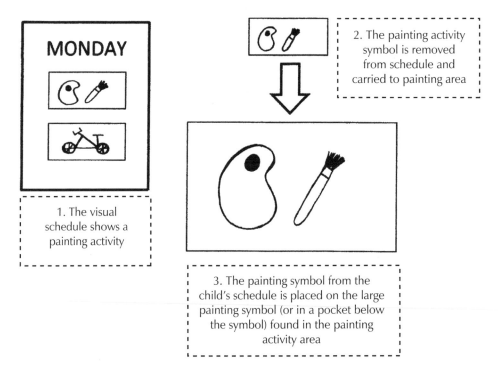

Figure 5.7: Baseboard Example

AMBER strategies (used to reinforce at bubbly times and bring back to GREEN) are below. The aim is to reduce demand at signs of stress by:

- Reducing language and communication (if using verbal commands reduce to a short phrase or single word, if using symbols or photos reduce to a single sign/gesture, symbol or photo swatch) to represent information. A portable white board or note pad can be used for this too.

- Giving *time and space* to calm (wait – don't nag).

- Adding in a short timed calming activity if needed and if appropriate to the situation (verbal or by using this–then).

AMBER also includes those times when we know there will be a difficult transition coming up (our AMBER warning!) such as a planned trip to the dentist or a holiday. GREEN strategies for the specific situation can be prepared in advance. For example, an individual can have a social story (pictorial or written) setting out what will happen, when, where and why it will happen and what will come next (see the list above). This can be accompanied by a pictorial travelling schedule or written list that the individual can take along and hold to remind and to reassure him or herself about what is happening. If there is time, photos of the place and of the people taken in advance are really helpful. If not, photos taken during the visit can be used next time and added to a richer social story and travelling schedule. An example of a travelling schedule for a fire drill can be found in Figure 5.8.

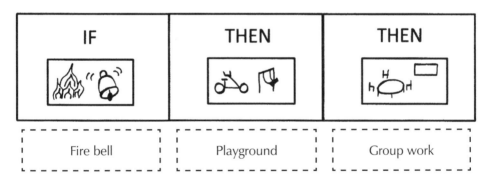

Figure 5.8: Travelling Schedule Example

CASE STUDY EXAMPLE: W

W has difficulties with longer transitions, that is, moving from one area to another. When she is anxious she may drop to the floor and refuse to move or may run back to where she came from.

GREEN strategies put in place to support transition are as follows:

- The transition is demonstrated right from the start of the day on the daily timetable or schedule (so that she can see it there during the day and get used to it).

- At time of transition a first, then and then card is used (see Figure 5.9). This shows what is happening now, what will happen next (the difficult transition) and what will happen after, (e.g. a snack, then PE (the difficult transition), then computer).

- Use of a personal CD player to listen to music on the way (this distracts and blocks out some of the noise during transition). There is a clear routine for storing the CD player in a 'safe box' as the next place is reached and the CD player stays there until the transition back.

- The journey is broken up by use of a timed (using a sand timer) rest stop (sitting on a bench in the garden area).

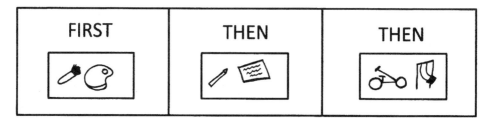

Figure 5.9: First, Then and Then

AMBER strategies, ready if there is a bubble, are as follows:

If W has dropped to the floor or run back to the classroom:

- She will be given time and space to calm. (Wait!)

- She will then be shown a choosing board (containing several things she likes to do) and a 'first–then' card. She can choose something she likes to put on the card for when the next session has finished (just in case the original reward was not motivating enough).

- She will be shown a sand timer and the transition will re-begin when the timer has finished.

RED: Should a RED behaviour occur (hitting out), this will be dealt with by saying 'Stop, hands down' and using a stop gesture, with a cold, calm and quiet voice and facial expression. Adults will, if possible, move away to give space to calm. A period of time out may be needed for more serious behaviour. Once calm (even for a short time), give a signal that now she is calm things can continue and then move to the AMBER strategies. Then back to GREEN.

Adapting according to age and ability

Whatever the age and ability of the individual concerned, the same principles and strategies can be used by adapting the level and type of communication, materials and resources used.

Developing skills and moving forward

We have seen how difficulty in managing transition and change generally stems from poor flexibility. Although we can alleviate some of the stress caused by transitions using strategies such as those above, and there is often some improvement in an individual's ability to manage particular transition and changes with familiarity and routine (back to structure and routine again!), flexibility skills tend not to simply appear without a focus on skill development.

As with all flexibility skills, movement along the flexibility continuum represents an individual's ability to learn and use new skills and to learn and use coping or self-management strategies. There therefore needs to be an emphasis on teaching and supporting the development of new flexibility skills (identified from the Flexibility Assessment) linked to transitioning such as tolerance of change, waiting and self-occupying, choice making and problem solving, planning and organising, predicting and anticipating, widening a range of interests, etc.

As described in Chapter 4, in addition to the teaching of new skills and self-management strategies, there is also a need to plan for generalisation and functional use of skills. This means making sure that the individual has the opportunity to use any new skills taught or developed *functionally*, that is strategies and skills learned for one transition are put into practical use across a range of transitions. This also means making sure that when we decide upon a strategy to support an individual we also look right from the start at how they might be able to use this independently and, if this isn't possible straight away, how we can support them to get to that stage.

Problem solving

In Chapter 1 we have seen how having difficulty with flexible thinking affects our ability to problem solve. Skills needed for successful problem solving are linked to both central coherence (our ability to make connections and see the whole picture) and to executive function (our ability to think, plan and do, organise and sequence). So why is problem solving, something we do every day, such a difficult process for someone with poor flexibility skills?

When solving a problem we encounter so many questions to answer (even though most of the time we don't realise we are answering them). For example:

- What exactly is the problem?

- Why is the problem happening?

- How do we solve it?

- What strategies could we use?

In addition there are choices and decisions and plans to make (what to do) and then once all these have been done, the process of carrying out the plan (how to do it) and finally solving the problem begins. Even then carrying out the plan is not that simple. As well as following steps through in sequence, problem solving requires regular reviewing and evaluation of progress which sometimes leads to adapting and refining the plan – we need to think about:

- What strategy or option would be best?

- How shall we set about solving the problem (carrying out the plan)?

- How do we know we are on the right track? Do we need to change?

- How do we know when we are successful?

- Could we have done things better (for next time)?

We encounter problems in every aspect of our lives; from simple problems (which we often don't even recognise as being problems) to more complex learning based or academic problems and to social problem solving. In Chapter 1, problems were placed into four main categories:

- social or emotional (and behaviour) problems

- learning, academic or intellectual problems

- everyday or personal problems

- physical problems.

So what knowledge and skills do we need in order to problem solve for all these purposes and to successfully work through all those steps above? We need to have a sense of purpose, to be goal orientated and work towards an end point (using our executive function). We need to know what that end point should be (Where do we want to get to? How will we know when the problem is solved? What will it look like?).

We need to have an overview of the whole process (getting the gist or using our central coherence) and the ability to put the details into place as the picture changes (i.e. flexibly applying strategies, trying things out and adapting approaches to gain success). All of this requires flexible thinking and adaptability and the ability to make choices and decisions and weigh up options.

We need to be able to evaluate the efficiency and effectiveness of the strategies used. This means being able to judge success by comparing where we are (what we are achieving) to where we want to get to (with our overall goal). Looking back at the areas commonly associated with flexibility as set out in Chapter 1 and comparing this to the list above, is there any wonder that problem solving can be an enormous task for those with flexibility problems?

The problem-solving process

Problem solving is a staged process in which we work through four main steps in order (even if we don't consciously think that we do). For simple everyday problems we are often unaware of following through stages because the processes have become so familiar and routine. Nonetheless they are there! To solve problems, we move through the four steps in sequence, each step adding more to the process of getting to our end point or finding a solution.

The four steps of problem solving are:

1. *Thinking:* Understanding the problem.

   This is the process of identifying and clarifying the details: what the problem is, what the elements of the problem are, why the problem occurs, what needs to be done to solve it (Where do I need to be? An analysis of what exactly needs to be done), what the end point will be (the goal).

   The need to have an overview of the problem is evident when we have more difficult problems to solve such as the car has a flat tyre – how do I get to the dentist on time? But for everyday problems to solve such as where do I sit? or What shall I wear? we move through this first step so quickly (we see the problem straight away) that we don't really notice it is there.

2. *Planning:* Developing solutions or action planning.

   This is where we use all the information from the first step to think about possible solutions (What do I need to do to get there?). For this we need to consider the options or choices that might be available (identifying the different ways of solving the problem) and then make a plan of how to go about solving the problem.

   Again, in many cases (such as in what shall I wear?), we simply make a choice and don't think that what we have done is to look at a number of options, taken the bigger picture into account (the weather, the event, etc.), made choices and then decided an end point (I'll wear a suit, which one?, the grey one, what shoes go with that?).

3. *Doing:* Carrying out the plan.

   Sometimes known as implementation, this is about working through the plan in a staged and systematic way (one step at a time).

   For this step we need to be able to do things in the right order (sequence) and work through to the end. This requires organisation and planning skills and the ability to stay on task.

4. *Reviewing:* Reviewing the situation.

   This is the evaluation stage. This again involves flexible thinking and also adaptability. As we move through the process of solving a problem, there is a need to stop and think and take account of how we are doing (our level of success, am I going off track?), making changes as and where they are needed to reach the end point. At the end, there is a need to look back at what you set out to do and judge your success against this (Did I get there? How well did I do?). This step also involves evaluating the success of the methods and strategies you used: Could another method have been easier? Or more successful? Or quicker, etc.?

Strategies and approaches to problem solving (GREEN)

When working with an individual with poor flexibility skills who finds problem solving difficult, there is often a temptation to solve the problem for them and tell them or show them what to do (or even do it for them). If, however, we want to support individuals to move along the flexibility continuum, develop problem-solving skills and strategies and develop their flexible thinking and independence, there is a need to provide support and teach skills and self-management strategies for each step of the problem-solving process. There are a number of strategies which can be used to support this. Examples of these are set out below.

1. Thinking – understanding the problem

This stage involves using strategies to set out the problem (this is the problem), to show the individual what the problem is (this is what it looks like) and help them to come to a conclusion about what the end point or outcome should be (this is where we need to be).

This process of identification and clarification can be supported by using techniques such as:

- Modelling: Making ideas concrete and showing relationships between elements of the problem. This could be making a 3D model to represent what the problem and the end point would look like (the car is broken, we need to fix it).

- Using pictures, photos or symbols to set out the problem. (It is raining – what shall we wear?)

- Drawing pictures, maps and diagrams. (We have these things and we need to make this, I have lots of toys – which do I choose to take on holiday?) An example is shown in Figure 5.10.

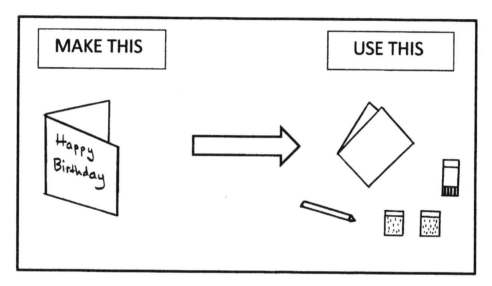

Figure 5.10: Make This – Use This

- Story boards or comic/cartoon strips. These are a sequence of pictures which set out a problem in story form and end with the end point (e.g. what should she do? I need to decide what to do next, etc.). These are particularly good for problem-solving behaviour issues. An example is shown in Figure 5.11.

This story board has been used to clarify the problem – i.e. *WHAT HAPPENED?* This could be used with a sad face or RED circle to show that this was not a good choice.

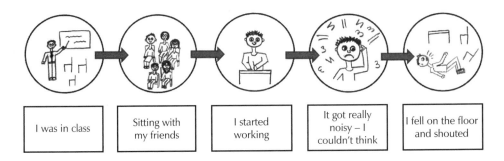

| I was in class | Sitting with my friends | I started working | It got really noisy – I couldn't think | I fell on the floor and shouted |

The same format can then be used to look at what the child *COULD DO*. This could be used with a smiley face or GREEN circle to show it is a good choice.

WHAT WOULD BE A BETTER CHOICE?

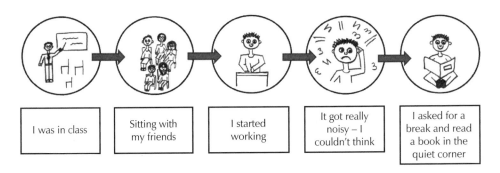

| I was in class | Sitting with my friends | I started working | It got really noisy – I couldn't think | I asked for a break and read a book in the quiet corner |

Figure 5.11: Story Board Examples

2. Planning – action planning (developing solutions)

The process of developing a solution to a plan is one of looking at the end point and thinking about possible ways of getting there. There are different ways of developing solutions, some more easily applied to some problems than others. For example:

- *Trial and error.* A simple form of problem solving which involves simply trying out different ways of solving the problem. For example, completion of a puzzle, getting bricks to fit into a box, etc.

- *Copycatting.* This involves seeing how someone else has solved the problem and copying that technique yourself.

- *Insight.* Simply 'suddenly' having an idea of what to do.

- *Choice makers.* These are spinners designed to aid decision making by matching problems to answers (e.g. What do I wear when it rains?). The arrow is pointed to the weather type (rain) and the other end of the arrow points to the answer (coat and umbrella). An example can be found in Figure 5.12.

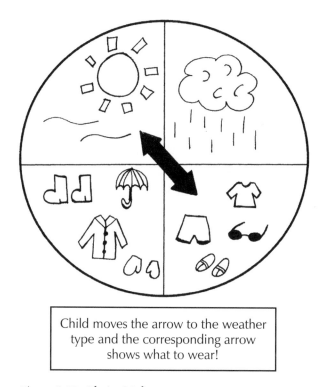

Child moves the arrow to the weather type and the corresponding arrow shows what to wear!

Figure 5.12: Choice Maker

- *Quick thinks.* This is where you think of all potential options, however creative! The latter however involves then making a choice about which option to choose. A technique useful for sorting 'quick thinks' and teaching the process of working through identifying options and choosing the right one is by using problem-solving pathways. Following *a problem-solving pathway* provides a structure to aid the decision making process and also incorporates Step 1, identifying the problem.

ABOUT THE PROBLEM-SOLVING PATHWAY

This provides a structured and visual method to help a child or young person to identify and solve problems. It can be adapted to suit any age and ability. In the initial stages, this is done jointly with the child or young person, with the key adult helping to establish the behaviour routine of following the path through and, if needed, providing some of the answers. The aim would be for the child or young person to gradually take more responsibility, until they are using the pathway independently. Steps 1 and 2 can be used flexibly and may be removed at later stages once routines are established. The problem-solving pathway and guidance is set out below. A blank problem-solving pathway and example of a completed pathway can be found in Figures 5.13 and 5.14.

- *Step 1: I have a problem!*

  This is the first step to independent problem solving, recognising that there is a problem and thinking calmly enough to move to the next stage. In some cases, it may be useful to link this to a relaxation or anger management routine (e.g. stop, think, count to 10).

- *Step 2: Where do I go? Who do I ask?*

  Ask and record or provide details about a safe place and/or key adult to go to for help.

- *Step 3: What is the problem?*

  The key adult supports the individual in describing what the problem is. If needed, drawings or comic/cartoon strips can be used to aid this.

- *Step 4: What could I do? (options)*

  Help the child/young person to consider possible solutions to the problem (you might need to think of some) and write them down (you can use post-it notes).

- *Step 5: My solution is…*

  Once all the options are written, go through each one talking through the pros and cons of choosing this option. Each time an option is rejected, cross it out or even tear it up. You are left with the solution!

- *And finally:* Write down the solution at the end (or place the post-it note in the answer box). If this is to be a long-term solution rather than a one off, the whole sequence can be kept as a problem pathway for that event and/ or can be written as a social story.

MY PROBLEM-SOLVING PATHWAY

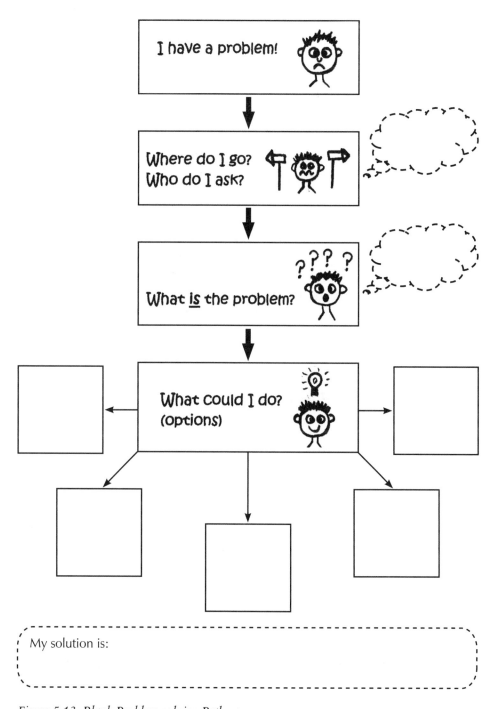

Figure 5.13: Blank Problem-solving Pathway

MY PROBLEM-SOLVING PATHWAY

I have a problem!

Where do I go?
Who do I ask?

Go to Mrs M in the office

What **is** the problem?

The playground is too noisy

Sit on the bench

X Still noisy

What could I do?
(options)

Run away

X NO! Too dangerous

Pull up my hood

X Still noisy

Sit in the library

YES!

Try to forget it

X Can't!

My solution is:

If the playground gets too noisy I will go to the library and read a book.

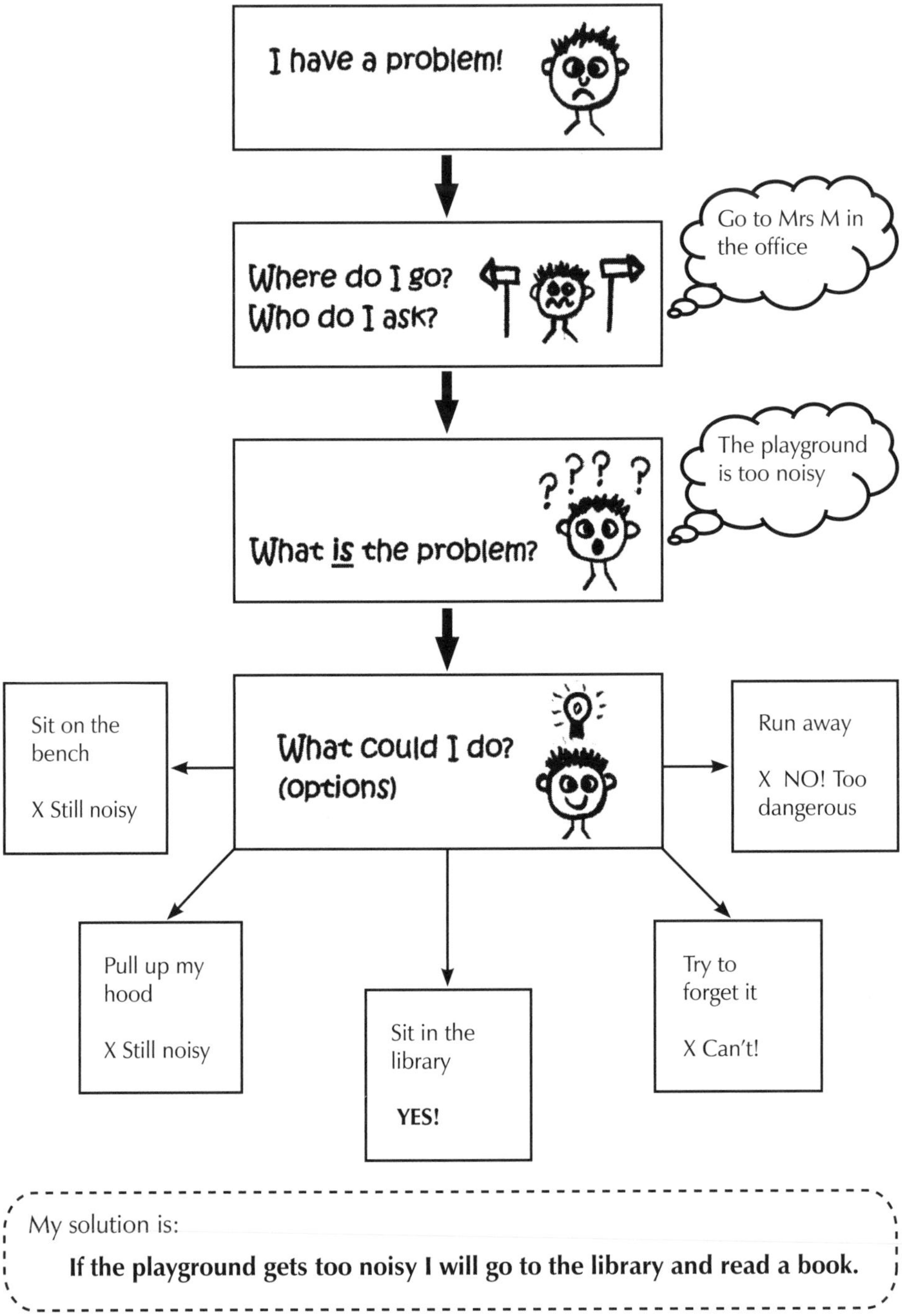

Figure 5.14: Problem-solving Pathway Example

3. Doing – carrying out a plan (implementation)

Once the solution is found, the next step is to work through the process to get to the end point. If the end point is a single action, as when using the problem-solving pathway above, this can simply be recorded and if support is needed, this can be put into a social story or flow chart to reinforce the process visually.

Visual strategies which support the individual to carry out a plan are as follows:

- flow charts, lists and diagrams

- maps and coloured route planners

- story boards or comic/cartoon strips (with solutions added)

- mini-schedules

- social stories and social sentences.

An example of a flow chart used for 'doing' can be found in Figure 5.15: Making a Cake. This can be extended by putting all the things to collect for the recipe and cooking process on one side of the card (things to collect) and the flow chart on the other (what to do).

4. Reviewing – reviewing the situation

This is the process of reviewing and evaluating and asking:

- What did I set out to do?

- What did I plan to do?

- What *did* I do?

- What did I finish with (the outcome)?

Techniques for supporting this include the use of photos and video (before, during and after), schedules, tick charts, recording, smiley/indifferent/sad faces, colour coding and so on. It is important to remember however that the process of reviewing and evaluating is also linked to the development of self-knowledge (see Chapter 6) and those supporting an individual through this part of the process should be mindful of their level of self-knowledge and ability to self-evaluate before asking them to make a difficult judgement such as rating, scoring or colour coding to estimate how they did.

MAKING A CAKE

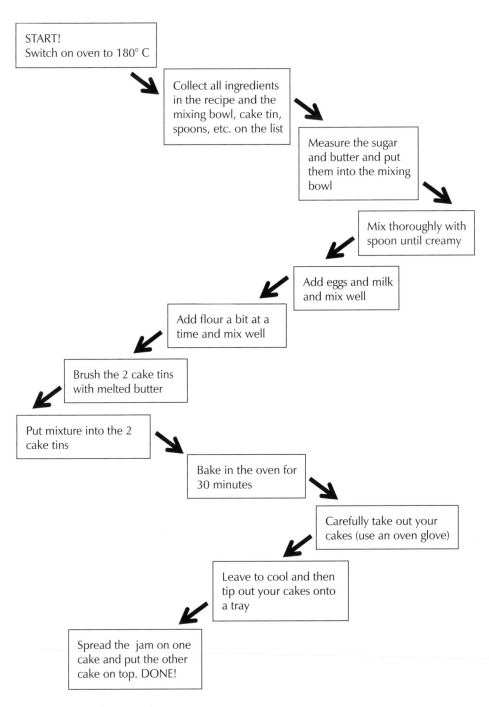

Figure 5.15: Making a Cake

Other GREEN strategies for the 'teacher'

Useful general strategies include:

- teaching choice and decision making

- teaching the individual to recognise the need for and ask for help

- make, and support the individual to make, connections with previous experiences

- make beginning and end points clear from the start

- explore different approaches and possible outcomes

- break tasks into clear definable steps

- support steps with prompt cards, checklists, diagrams, etc.

- model or picture the final expected outcome.

Rigid problem solving: Those supporting an individual with problem solving should also remember that those with poor flexibility may have a tendency towards rigidity. In other words you might teach a problem-solving technique or a solution to a problem and this may either become the norm, a strategy which is adopted as a rule regardless of context, or may only be used in the one situation taught and not generalised into everyday use. This can be alleviated by teaching flexibility skills and providing a range of opportunity to use and develop skills (see Chapter 7).

Sabotage! To encourage problem-solving skill development and prevent rigid patterns arising, sabotage is a good strategy. This means changing the usual routine and leaving something out so that there is a need to think of another solution. For example: painting a picture and the blue paint has run out, building a train set but there is a piece missing, needing to cut but no scissors, a spoon too big for the yoghurt and so on. How much of a problem you present depends on the ability and skill level of the individuals concerned (this should not cause stress). Adults should adopt an approach of supporting the problem-solving process (this may mean that you give the answer in the first instance), gradually giving prompts until the individual can solve the problems him or herself.

Thinking, planning and doing in other contexts

As can be seen in Chapter 1, Step 3 of the problem-solving process, the ability to plan, organise and sequence or to think, plan and do, requires good executive function skills. Difficulties in this area in particular are common within individuals presenting with a range of disorders such as ADHD, Asperger's Syndrome and Dyspraxia and are also common as a stand alone problem where there appears to be no other learning or social issue.

In my experience, this aspect of flexibility is frequently overlooked or the difficulties underestimated, particularly where an individual appears to have the separate skills he or she needs to do all the parts of a task or action. It is important to remember therefore that it is the following through the process or series of steps that is the problem.

Individuals who experience, think, plan and do (executive function) difficulties may show an inconsistency in their performance. For example they may be able to read, talk and spell really well but then cannot write a story or answer written questions for a task. The difference here is the number of steps involved. Even if you can read and write it may be hard to read the questions, think about the answer (problem solve), think about how to put this down into coherent prose and then work through the process of actually writing it down in that order.

If an individual struggles with complex, multi-staged tasks but has all the separate skills needed to complete it, this may well point to difficulties with executive function and flexible thinking. It is easy to make a link then with behaviour problems and low self-esteem, particularly if expectations and demands placed upon them are unrealistic.

These difficulties similarly apply to social and personal tasks and situations such as personal organisation skills and social problem solving. Again having the separate skills you need to dress, bathe, pack your bag and get everything ready for school on time does not necessarily mean that you have the executive function skills you need to put this together into a process and within a given timeframe. Having the social skills you need to communicate and negotiate with others, the ability to talk about the social rules and the ability to analyse afterwards what you should have done, does not necessarily mean that you have the skills to work through a difficult social situation at the time and in the right way (social problem solving).

This is where the Flexibility Assessment and knowing the individual well (good observation in a number of settings and activities) comes in. Individuals identified as having difficulties with thinking and planning will still require specific support and strategies as set out within this chapter, adapted according to their level of ability and level of flexibility.

Strategies can include:

- Reducing the number of processes involved in a task (scaffolding or staging a task).

- Supporting the individual to recognise, verbalise and record the processes involved in some of the more complex tasks (e.g. structuring stories) and take him or herself step by step through the rules of how to tackle problems and problem solve.

- Some pre-teaching of sequences of cueing instructions will help to develop independence and confidence in task organisation and completion (lists of instructions for a task perhaps put in pictorial form).

Useful visual strategies include:

- task lists, checklists and written timetables

- diaries and planners (electronic or paper!)

- post-it notes and reminder books or to do lists

- diagrams, maps and flow charts

- spider diagrams and mind or concept maps (e.g. Buzan 2003)

- colour coding and highlighting

- visual problem-solving strategies (pathways, etc.).

Adaptability

As seen in Chapter 1, rigidity, ritualistic behaviour and difficulty with adaptability is commonly associated with poor flexibility. In many circumstances, the problems and strategies set out in the sections on transitions and on problem solving will be the same. However, there are some behaviours resulting from rigidity (and the anxiety associated with this) which cause slightly different problems and therefore require slightly different strategies. For example: I always do this – this way – with this person (I am not going to change). I always have this toy, I always sit on this seat, I am always first and so forth.

Often these behaviours are seen as the individual wanting control and always wanting their own way. This is true to a certain extent but the inference is often that this is a deliberate (and therefore negative) behaviour rather than the need for control and adherence to the rigid routine being a strategy for reducing stress, and controlling the environment and staying in familiar territory. Individuals with poor flexibility who insist on control do so because they lack the skills they need to manage changing circumstances (adaptability). It is safer and less stressful to stick with what you know!

GREEN strategies

There are a number of GREEN strategies which can be used to support individuals who find it hard to let go of rigid routines and rituals, to the extent that they create barriers to learning. These include strategies to limit the time or number of rituals such as the use of visual (e.g. sand timers), using countdowns (4 more, 3 more,

2 more, etc.), counting (3 times then stop). Strategies to support transitions as listed earlier in this chapter are also useful.

The use of social stories (Gray 2002) or picture stories can help to set out a picture of what happens if there is a change (e.g. usually we go this way to school but sometimes we have to pick up Tom and if this happens we go a different way but we get there in the end). Similarly 'first–then' cards can be used in these circumstances.

Teaching 'surprise' *in advance* is also a useful strategy. This can be identified by use of a particular symbol or picture to denote a sudden change and used alongside 'first–then–then' cards to show what will happen after the surprise. Teaching a sudden change in this way can start with a pleasant surprise (surprise: we are having computer), building up to more stressful change such as a change of adult or room or the fire alarm. If there are regular unplanned surprises such as a change of teacher or staff or a fire alarm, there can be preparation beforehand with use of a social story or photo story to set out what happens and why and what you are going to do. These can be ready to give alongside the surprise message to reinforce the scenario and reduce stress. Travelling schedules depicting the route and process for fire drill can be kept ready for when the moment comes (see Figure 5.8).

Other strategies include:

- *Turn-taking strips* (example Figure 5.16): These provide photos or names of the individual and friends which are put in order according to the turn-taking rota. The person having their turn is placed at the front and, once the turn is taken, they go to the back of the list and the next person moves up. The individual can be in charge of moving the people along the line. This gives some control, even if they cannot control when it is their turn.

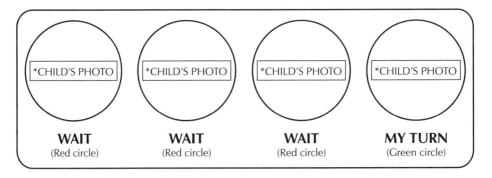

Each time an individual has a turn (on the GREEN circle) their photo is removed and placed at the end of the line. Photos are moved along the line towards GREEN to give a visual reminder of when your turn is coming! This process can be controlled by the 'teacher' or by the individuals themselves according to level of ability and understanding.

Figure 5.16: Turn-Taking Strip

- *Colours or labels.* These can be used for occasions such as lining up or sitting on chairs. Each individual can have a colour or animal/car, etc. which always shows where they sit or stand (keeping some rigidity). These can then be changed and reordered (or the individual can take a turn in putting out the order). Photo and name cards can also be used.

- *Choice making hats and spinners:* Pulling names (or photos) out of hats, spinners and dice games can also be used to order or select pairs, groups, etc. These can also be used to select toys, games, activities to widen interests and avoid sticking to the same routine. These can then be put in order.

- *Ordering choices or timetable.* At times where some flexibility in order of activity is possible, the individual can select the order in which things occur and put them on their timetable or choice board (you have to do this but you can choose in what order).

All of the above strategies support the development of flexibility and adaptability but also allow the individual some control. This serves to reduce stress levels and develop independence. In formal settings, at times we are able to give free choice but often there is no choice that something has to be done. Where we can though, we should be able to offer some control about when, what order, or how or who with.

CASE STUDY EXAMPLE: D

D has difficulty with turn taking. D really likes the pirate game and plays this within a group of four others. But once he has had his turn, he becomes really anxious about when he will get another turn and worries when someone else has a turn. He may snatch the game or even hurt the peer taking their turn.

GREEN strategies

There are photos of everyone involved in the game. A turn-taking strip (Figure 5.16) is used. The GREEN circle on the strip means it is your turn (GO!). The RED circles mean wait (until it is your turn). When D has finished his turn, he moves his photo onto the RED circle at the back of the strip and moves the next person along to have their go. He can see when his turn is coming and has some control over the turn taking even if he can't change the order.

This can be adapted for a more able group by making use of a basket-ball or team game scenario where players may move to a waiting area until called for their turn.

AMBER strategies

If D shows signs of becoming anxious, before it is his turn, he is reminded of the turn-taking strip and prompted to count the people before him. He is allowed to hold a small item from the game while he waits. A sand timer can also be used to give him a break from the table if waiting gets too much (using 'first break then back to game').

RED strategies

Should a RED behaviour occur (snatching or hitting out), this will be dealt with by saying 'Stop, hands down' and using a stop gesture, a cold, calm and quiet voice and facial expression. Adults will, if possible, move away to give space to calm. Time out may be needed for more serious behaviour. Once calm (even for a short time), give a signal that now he is calm things can continue and then move to the AMBER strategies. Then back to GREEN.

References

Buzan, T. (2003) *Mind Maps for Kids – an Introduction.* London: Thorsons.

Gray, C. (2002) *My Social Story Book.* London and Philadelphia: Jessica Kingsley Publishers.

Chapter Six

'DO YOU WANT TO KNOW WHAT I THINK?'

Flexibility, independence, self-advocacy and participation

Over recent years there has been an increased emphasis on the process of participation – enabling children and young people and giving them a voice. This means we involve children and young people in making decisions which affect them and their well-being and we listen to and take account of their views.

This chapter takes a look at the process of participation and the role that flexibility plays in this. It explores the close interrelationship between flexibility, self-knowledge and self-expression. In addition to the 5P Approach Flexibility Assessment introduced in Chapter 3, this chapter introduces two other related assessment tools, the 5P Approach Assessment of Self-knowledge and the 5P Approach Expressing Views Assessment.

Why participation?

Enabling participation provides adults with access to children and young people's ideas and points of view. It allows adults to gain an understanding of the child or young person's perspective and provides opportunities to develop shared understanding between them. It also provides opportunities for the development of language and communication skills, self-awareness and social skills and provides opportunity for choice and decision making, for learning about responsibility and the development of independence.

For individuals with communication difficulty however this often presents problems and, whatever the underlying cause of those difficulties, enabling participation can be a challenging task. Finding the right way of asking their opinion or at times even understanding what an individual is seeking (however able) can be difficult. For those who present with behaviour difficulty or signs of anxiety and distress, understanding them and what they are trying to convey is a major element in solving problems and meeting their needs (creating a GREEN Zone). Giving them a voice is therefore crucial.

There is little doubt that enabling pupil participation is the *morally* right thing to do, and in addition there are legal obligations and guidelines which support this. Since the emergence of the Children Act in 1989 there has been a steady stream of guidance and legal requirements all relating to enabling participation in children and young people. This includes the following:

- The Children Act (1989)

- United Nations Convention on the Rights of the Child (ratified in UK, December 1999)

- Human Rights Act 1998 (in force in UK, October 2000)

- SEN and Disability Act (2001)

- Revised Code of Practice for SEN (DfES 2001)

- ASD Guidelines for Good Practice (DfES and DoH 2002)

- SEN Update 14a (Removing the Barriers, DfES 2004b)

- Every Child Matters (DfES 2004a)

- Pupil Participation and Pupil Voice (DfES 2004c)

- Citizenship and the Assessment for Learning Strategy (Department for Children, Schools and Families 2008).

In response, schools, professionals and organisations have steadily developed guidelines, resources and techniques for involving children and young people as much as possible in decisions which affect them and in obtaining and listening to their views. However as we have seen, for children and young people with disability or special educational need, this is often no easy task.

The Human Rights Act, The SEN and Disability Act (2001), and Revised Code of Practice for Special Educational Needs (DfES 2001) all make it clear that the views of children and young people whatever their needs or ability must be sought and taken into account in decision-making processes and that they should play an active role in planning and evaluating learning targets. In particular, The Revised Code of Practice, the legal framework currently used for guiding the education of those with special educational needs, states that the views of students with special educational needs should be sought at all reviews and within the statutory assessment process itself.

Children, who are capable of forming views, have a right to receive and make known information, to express an opinion, and to have that opinion taken in to account on any matters affecting them. The views of the child should be given due weight according to the age, maturity and capability of the child.

Taken from 'Enabling Pupil Participation', SEN Toolkit – Section 4, Revised Code of Practice for SEN (DfES 2001, p.3)

This is supported further in SEN Update 14 (DfES 2004b) which includes action to publish 'practical tools for involving young people with SEN and disabilities in decisions about their learning' (p. 67).

Specifically related to Autistic Spectrum Disorder, the ASD Guidelines for Good Practice (DfES and DoH 2002) includes a section on advocacy with practical pointers for schools and local authorities.

There are clearly many implications for schools and organisations working with children and young people with special educational needs. Legislation makes it clear that schools have a duty to seek the views of their students in matters which affect them and to involve them in decision-making processes. This should not just be a matter of asking children and young people their views in relation to special needs targets and reviews, but points to a change in the way we view student participation within school. Many schools have developed student councils in order to obtain student views on school issues which affect them and to involve them in decision-making processes.

About participation

Participation therefore is not just the process of allowing children and young people to express their views on matters which affect them but involves the whole process of developing independence, providing opportunity, listening, taking views into account and creating a culture where participation is the norm.

The principle of enabling pupil participation therefore applies to *all*, but the level at which children and young people participate will vary from individual to individual according to age, maturity and skills. Degree of participation may also vary according to individual circumstances or the decision to be made. For example children within a primary school may be given a relatively free choice to voice an opinion on the range of small toys within the playground but less involvement in the decisions about planning a school trip.

Not all children and young people, therefore, can make decisions about and take responsibility for all aspects affecting their lives, but they may all be able to be *involved* even at the lowest level. There is a fine balance to be drawn between ensuring that pupils are encouraged to participate as fully as possible and ensuring that they are not overwhelmed and overburdened by being given more responsibility than they can cope with – or that encouraging participation becomes a token gesture. Roller (1998) considers enabling pupil participation to be about informing pupils, consulting with them and allowing them choice.

Gersch (1987) suggests that there should be a 'continuum of participation' allowing each individual to be involved at their own level. This also introduces the notion that children may progress along the continuum as they mature and develop new skills and understanding. In practice, this is often what happens as children grow and develop from early childhood into teenagers and then to young adults.

Over the years, several models have evolved suggesting that there can be degrees of participation. Shier (2001) sets out a pathway to participation with five stages which increase in degree or amount of participation, and Alderson and Montgomery (1996) suggest that children can be consulted at four levels also gradually increasing in level of participation. Using these examples as a base, a continuum of participation could include the following four levels:

1. Being informed and listened to.

2. Supported involvement (i.e. supported to express views and have these taken into account).

3. Involvement in decision making (being given a choice).

4. Fully involved (sharing responsibility).

Participation skills and flexibility

So what does enabling participation have to do with flexibility? What then are the barriers to participation for children and young people with autism and related disorders or those with flexibility difficulties?

In order to participate in matters which affect them, all children and young people require some key skills. These include:

- the ability to listen, understand others and to communicate

- the ability to relay information on thoughts, beliefs and desires

- the ability to make choices

- knowledge about themselves

- the ability to relay information about themselves

- the ability to reflect on their own learning and behaviour

- the ability to reflect on the implications their decisions and choices may have on themselves and others.

These can be summarised into the following three areas, or a participation triad, all of which overlap and interrelate.

1. *Involvement* – the skills, understanding and motivation to become involved in decision-making processes (adaptability), the ability to apply and generalise skills for differing purposes (flexibility).

2. *Self-awareness* – the ability to understand and identify needs and to self-evaluate (to understand yourself and others).

3. *Communication and self-expression* – the ability to understand information given, what is expected and the ability to express a view (in addition to the language skills needed this requires the ability to think, plan, do and review).

These are all skills identified within the Flexibility Elements (Figure 1.1) in Chapter 1 and skills which those with poor flexibility often find difficult. There is therefore a direct link between enabling children and young people to participate in decision making and to express their views and flexibility of thought. The three Flexibility Assessment areas – Play and Social Development, Thinking and Conceptual Understanding, and Adaptability – all contain skills which relate to the areas identified above such as understanding yourself and others, understanding ambiguous concepts, being adaptable and using skills flexibly to make choices and problem solve.

Enabling participation and giving a voice to children and young people therefore means more than asking them what they think and simply providing them with a means to communicate. They also need support to learn more about themselves, their likes and dislikes and their feelings. They need support to develop independence, to make choices and decisions and to problem solve. They need to develop skills in these areas and to be given the opportunity to practise and use emerging skills. A central part of the process is to enable them to develop self-knowledge and acquire the skills and flexibility they need to become more independent in thought, learning and behaviour.

This process however is one of gradual skill development over time. If we look back at the Flexibility Continuum in Table 2.2, we can see the link between developing flexibility skills and developing independence. As individuals move along the flexibility continuum, their independence also increases as does their ability to use their skills flexibly in situations where they are required to participate in decision making and to express a view (the basis of a participation continuum?). The 5P Approach Flexibility Assessment therefore provides a framework for assessing and developing one of the three key skill areas relating to participation.

Developing self-knowledge

The Flexibility Elements and the 5P Approach Flexibility Assessment contain statements which relate directly to skills which support the development of self-knowledge. For example, Play and Social Development includes looking at the understanding of others and of emotions. These are skills needed in order to develop an understanding of oneself as a person.

The development of self-knowledge and the development of flexibility therefore interrelate and share much common ground. However, in order to fully support the development of self-knowledge, there is a need to look at this in finer detail. The 5P Approach Assessment of Self-knowledge has been developed to expand on those self-knowledge areas identified within the 5P Approach Flexibility Assessment and to look in more detail at the *second* skill area relating to participation: self-knowledge.

The 5P Approach Assessment of Self-knowledge

The development of self-knowledge or self-awareness is recognised as an area of difficulty for children and young people with autism and within many other related disorders. Difficulties in this area relate to the underlying features of an individual's diagnosis – flexibility of thought, and poor Theory of Mind, and have frequently been the focus of interest and research in the field of autism (e.g. Baron-Cohen 1997). Difficulties with Theory of Mind – the ability to understand oneself and to understand others' minds and intentions – is a core feature of autism (known as part of the autistic cognitive style). In order to understand other people, however, you also need to have an understanding of yourself as a person or to have self-knowledge. This is therefore a priority area for intervention for those with autism and related disorders.

Self-knowledge (or having a self-concept) develops with the steady accumulation of a wide range of knowledge about oneself such as physical characteristics, personality, abilities, beliefs and values. The development of self-knowledge in children is complex and begins at a very early stage and progresses through several stages – for example from copying others to recognising yourself in the mirror, from knowing about your physical characteristics to understanding the effect that your behaviour has on others, and reflecting on your own behaviour and comparing yourself to others. Developing all of these skills however also requires an ability to make choices, to problem solve and to make connections with previous experiences – in other words, the ability to think flexibly. This clearly demonstrates the very close link between flexibility and the development of self-knowledge.

Developing self-knowledge is closely linked with the development of social skills and self-expression (expressing a view) and by implication therefore to independence, pupil voice and to self-advocacy.

The 5P Approach Assessment of Self-knowledge provides a basis for a formative and summative assessment of self-knowledge skills relating to pupil participation. Areas chosen for this assessment tool form a developmental scale or continuum and focus specifically on those areas of self-knowledge which relate to flexible thinking and independence and those in which individuals with autism and related disorders often experience difficulty. This assessment also provides a means of identifying targets and monitoring progress within an area which is often not included within traditional curriculum-based assessments.

The structure of this assessment is broadly similar to the 5P Approach Flexibility Assessment. As in the Flexibility Assessment, the level of skill development within each distinct area of the 5P Approach Assessment of Self-knowledge is graded from 1: not present to 5: established.

The 5P Approach Assessment of Self-knowledge comprises:

- The Self-knowledge Continuum

- The Self-knowledge Checklist

- The Self-knowledge Quick Reference Summary Chart

- The Self-knowledge Assessment Summary.

The Self-knowledge Continuum

Based on models proposed by Neisser (1997) and Damon and Hart (1991), this continuum has been constructed to broadly follow the developmental progression of self-knowledge from the early stages of identifying concrete characteristics to a more abstract understanding of psychological characteristics, thoughts and feelings and how these interrelate with others. The continuum identifies five broad areas which follow this developmental pathway: A: self-definition and physical self, B: complex information about self, C: social self (self in social situations), D: self as a learner, E: self-evaluation and self-reflection. These are further broken down into key skills within each stage, again broadly following a developmental pathway (see Figure 6.1).

It should be noted however that although the development of self-knowledge follows a developmental pathway which increases in skill complexity, many individuals and particularly those with social communication difficulty may demonstrate some more complex skills even though earlier skills have not been fully accomplished. This assessment therefore allows for separate scoring of the five areas of the continuum and for the individual skills within them. This not only gives a better overview of self-knowledge skills but enables identification of areas for intervention to fill the gaps.

Developmental pathway

→

1. Physical self and self-definition	2. Complex information about self	3. Social self (self in social situations)	4. Self as a learner	5. Self-evaluation and reflection

Self-knowledge Continuum Areas – Skills

A. Self-definition and self-awareness (What am I like?)	B. Complex information about self (What kind of person am I?)
Skills:	Skills:
Awareness of physical/sensory needs	Preferences (likes and dislikes)
Behavioural expression of feelings/emotions	Feelings (recognition and understanding)
Recognition of own actions on environment (e.g. cause and effect toys)	Recognition of the consequences of own actions/behaviour
Early self-definition (e.g. recognising self, name, possessions, etc.)	Personality traits
	Self-interest
Developing self-recognition (e.g. basic information about self – hair colour, etc.) (i.e. All about me)	Differences to others
	Self in past and future
C. Social self (Me and others) *Linked to Theory of Mind development*	**D. Self as a learner (Me as a learner)**
Skills:	Skills:
Interest in others	Identifying preferences for activities
Tolerance of others	Identifying preferences for learning (style)
Shared attention	Asking for help
Sharing (with adult and child)	Accepting help/direction
Following social cues and direction (from adult and child)	Organisation/independence
Imitation of others (adults and peers)	**E. Self-evaluation and self-reflection (How do I do?)**
Responding appropriately to others (adults and peers)	Skills:
Approaching others for interaction/help/comfort, etc.	Identifying skills
Adapting response to different people/situations	Identifying strengths
	Identifying difficulties/weaknesses
Demonstrating empathy	Evaluation of success
	Suggestions for improvement
	Recognition and analysis of mistakes

Figure 6.1: The Self-Knowledge Continuum

About the Self-knowledge Checklist

As set out in the introduction, the 5P Approach Self-knowledge Checklist provides a means of recording individual skills on a scale of 1–5. Scores given are based on observation and the subjective judgement of those who know the individual best. The aim is to record only skills and progress which are functional, persistent, and demonstrated over time rather than information simply obtained from a one off assessment or observation. Completion of this document is therefore best done through a range of methods, by including someone who knows the child or young person well or in discussion with those who do, through a series of observations, and through use of specifically planned activities (see the assessment activity and resources guidance after each section below) which prompt the use of self-knowledge skills.

Note: If planned activities are used for this purpose, it is important to ensure that any conclusion drawn reflects established or persistent use of skills rather than a single success or failure.

Using the Self-knowledge Checklist

The Self-knowledge Checklist can be found in Table 6.1. Using the five areas of the Self-knowledge Continuum as its basis, this checklist identifies key skills within each area in a broadly developmental order, each skill being scored separately and each area scored separately.

Where to start? The first step is to provide a baseline. Each area comprises several statements describing behaviour which represents a self-knowledge skill. Progression within skill areas is broadly developmental. As in the 5P Approach Flexibility Assessment, each statement is given a score of 1–5 (not present – established as below) in the assessed level of achievement column according to the level of skill development to date. Guidance for the Score Descriptors is as for the 5P Approach Flexibility Assessment and can be found in Table 3.4.

A total for each self-knowledge area is calculated and recorded at the bottom of the page. In order to monitor progress across a year, the Self-knowledge Checklist has capacity for both baseline (B) and termly assessment (record in T1, T2, T3). These totals are then recorded on the Self-knowledge Assessment Summary to provide an overview.

Table 6.1 The Self-knowledge Checklist

A. Self-definition and self-awareness (What am I like?)

Key Skills	Assessed Level of Achievement				Example: How does s/he show this?	Person/s contributing to assessment
	B	T1	T2	T3		
Shows an awareness of physical and sensory needs (rejects, seeks and/or requests)						
Gives a behavioural expression of feelings and/or emotions						
Recognises the effect of his/her actions on the environment (e.g. on cause and effect toys)						
Recognises the effect of his/her actions on people (e.g. smiles, hugs, hurt, etc.)						
Demonstrates early self-definition (e.g. recognising self, possessions, etc.)						
Shows developing self-recognition (e.g. shows a knowledge of basic information about self. i.e. hair colour, name, etc.) (All about me)						
TOTAL	30	30	30	30		

Key: 1 = Not present
        2 = Emerging
        3 = Developing skills
        4 = Using new skills
        5 = Established

B. Complex information about self (What kind of person am I?)

Key Skills	Assessed Level of Achievement				Example: How does s/he show this?	Person/s contributing to assessment
	B	T1	T2	T3		
Identifies preferences/likes						
Identifies dislikes						
Identifies/recognises own feelings						
Understands/attributes reason for feelings						
Recognises the consequences of own actions or behaviour						
Identifies personality traits and personal qualities						
Demonstrates self-interest (uses 'I')						
Recognises own differences to others (e.g. I like, s/he likes)						
Is able to think back (i.e. place self in past)						
Is able to think forward (i.e. place self in future)						
TOTAL	—50	—50	—50	—50		

Key:

> 1 = Not present
> 2 = Emerging
> 3 = Developing skills
> 4 = Using new skills
> 5 = Established

continued

C. Social self (Me and others) *Note: Linked to Theory of Mind development*

Key Skills	Assessed Level of Achievement				Example: How does s/he show this?	Person/s contributing to assessment
	B	T1	T2	T3		
Shows an interest in others						
Shows tolerance of others						
Establishes shared attention						
Demonstrates sharing (with adult and/or child)						
Follows social cues and direction (from adult and/or child)						
Demonstrates imitation of others (adults and/or peers)						
Responds appropriately to others (adults and/or peers)						
Approaches others (adult or peer) for interaction help/comfort, etc.						
Adapts behaviour to different people or situations						
Demonstrates empathy (towards adults or peers)						
TOTAL	50	50	50	50		

Key:

1 = Not present
2 = Emerging
3 = Developing skills
4 = Using new skills
5 = Established

D. Self as a learner (Me as a learner)

Key Skills	Assessed Level of Achievement				Example: How does s/he show this?	Person/s contributing to assessment
	B	T1	T2	T3		
Identifies preferences for activities – behavioural						
Identifies preferences for activities – makes a choice						
Identifies preferences for learning – behavioural						
Identifies preferences for learning – makes a choice						
Recognises role as a learner (i.e. understands and follows routine and structure of lesson)						
Identifies need for help						
Asks for help						
Accepts help/direction						
Shows organisation/independence skills (in learning)						
Shows organisation/independence skills (personal)						
TOTAL	50	50	50	50		

Key:

1 = Not present
2 = Emerging
3 = Developing skills
4 = Using new skills
5 = Established

continued

The 5P Approach

E. Self-evaluation and self-reflection (How do I do?)

Key Skills	Assessed Level of Achievement				Example: How does s/he show this?	Person/s contributing to assessment
	B	T1	T2	T3		
Identifies skills achieved (I can)						
Identifies strengths (I am good at)						
Identifies difficulties/weaknesses (I can't – I need help with)						
Evaluates level of success – learning (rating)						
Evaluates level of success – behaviour (rating)						
Makes suggestions for improvement (targets, goals) – learning						
Makes suggestions for improvement (targets, goals) – behaviour						
Recognises and analyses mistakes – learning						
Recognises and analyses mistakes – behaviour						
TOTAL	45	45	45	45		

Key:
1 = Not present
2 = Emerging
3 = Developing skills
4 = Using new skills
5 = Established

The SP Approach

Recording observations and skill achievement

The 5P Approach Self-knowledge Checklist also has a section for recording an example of how the child or young person displays that s/he has acquired the skill (in the column 'How does s/he show this?'). This should be completed when a score of 5 is achieved giving a concrete example of how the skill has been demonstrated. For best practice, skill acquisition can also be recorded through photo or video which is cross referenced under the relevant item. Examples of what type of skill or behaviour would be observed for each of the statements in the 5P Approach Self-knowledge Checklist are set out in a completed checklist in Table 6.2.

The Self-knowledge Assessment Yearly Summary

This can be found in Table 6.3. This summary provides a visual summative profile for the individual mapping the acquisition of self-knowledge skills and for plotting progress throughout the year. It provides a means of identifying skill achievement for each of the five areas of the Self-knowledge Checklist. It provides a means of identifying overall totals within each of the five Self-knowledge Checklist areas and is constructed to provide a means of measuring and recording progress on a termly basis from an initial baseline score.

Total, Baseline or T1, 2 or 3 scores obtained are placed under the appropriate Area column (A B C D E) along with a percentage score (calculated separately using the formula: raw score ÷ total score × 100).

The numerical and percentage scoring system used provides a means of measuring small step progress within each area. The numerical scores can also be placed into a database to plot progress over a greater length of time and to allow comparison of degree of progress across individuals or across groups. An example of a completed Self-knowledge Assessment Yearly Summary Sheet can be found in Table 6.4.

The Self-knowledge Quick Reference Summary Chart

This *optional* chart is used in conjunction with the Self-knowledge Checklist and provides a quick reference overview of all the individual skills within the five areas of the checklist. Scores obtained from the checklist assessment are plotted on the quick reference chart under the appropriate headings. A copy of this chart can be found in Table 6.5.

Table 6.2 Recording Self-knowledge Observations and Skill Achievement Example

The 5P Approach Self-knowledge Checklist also has a section for recording an example of how the child or young person displays that s/he has acquired the skill. This should be completed when a score of 5 is given giving a concrete example of how the skill has been demonstrated. For best practice, skill acquisition can also be recorded through photo or video which is cross referenced under the relevant item. Examples of what type of skill or behaviour would be observed for each of the statements in the 5P Approach Self-knowledge Checklist are set out below.

ELEMENT: SELF-DEFINITION AND SELF-AWARENESS (What am I like?)

Key Skills	Example: How would s/he show this?
Shows an awareness of physical and sensory needs	Rejects, seeks and/or requests food or drink, physical activity or clothing (too hot, too cold, too itchy!), sensory toys and activities, etc.
Shows a behavioural expression of feelings and/or emotions	Observer is able to identify emotional state/feelings of child or young person through clear behavioural signs (e.g. facial expression, crying, laughter, running away, hiding, excitement, etc.).
Recognises the effect of his/her actions on the environment (e.g. on cause and effect toys)	Shows an understanding of *their role* in cause and effect by use of cause and effect toys, throwing toys, tipping over brick towers, etc.
Recognises the effect of his/her actions on people	Shows an understanding that they can make an action which has an effect on others (e.g. smiles, hugs, hurting, will take a symbol to request, etc.)
Demonstrates early self-definition (e.g. recognising self, possessions, etc.)	Recognises self in mirror, knows which things are their possessions (toys, clothes, etc.). Responds to name (turns or comes when called). Will pick out a picture of themselves from a selection, on a school notice board, etc.
Shows developing self-recognition	Is able to show a knowledge of basic information about self through verbal means, sign or symbol choice (e.g. hair colour, name, sex, etc.)

Self-definition and self-awareness (What am I like?): Assessment and resources

Assessment through observation in a range of setting and/or discussion with person who knows the child or young person well. Interactive play sessions are also useful (i.e. intensive interaction sessions, turn-taking and physical play activities). Useful resources include

- a range of simple cause and effect toys (e.g. toys with switches, buttons to push, noisy toys, bricks for tower building, etc.)
- mirror, photos of child and others
- all about me book, symbols for hair colour, boy/girl, name card, etc.

ELEMENT: COMPLEX INFORMATION ABOUT SELF (What kind of person am I?)

Key Skills	Example: How would s/he show this?
Identifies preferences	Able to select toy/food item (make a choice) s/he prefers
Identifies dislikes	Able to reject toy/food item (make a choice) s/he prefers
Identifies own feelings (recognition)	Identifies (correctly!) that s/he is happy, sad, angry, etc. through verbal means, sign or symbol choice
Understands/attributes reason for feelings	Able to understand and communicate 'I am happy because…', 'I am sad because…' through verbal, sign or symbol means – including making a choice from a selection of reasons
Recognises consequences of own actions/behaviour	Shows an understanding that there is a consequence to their behaviour (e.g. finishing a task to get to the next, gaining reward, missing a turn/activity, making someone sad or angry, etc.) Demonstrates behaviourally, verbally, through sign or symbol
Identifies personality traits/personal qualities	Will identify personality traits and qualities (correctly!) such as kind, helpful, friendly, etc. Through verbal means, sign or symbol (from a choice if needed)
Demonstrates self-interest	Uses 'I' or first name to show a personal interest or opinion
Recognises differences to others	Shows an understanding that others have different views and feelings (e.g. I like, s/he likes)
Able to place self in past	Shows an ability to think back or reflect on past experiences e.g. 'when we went to the park', 'last time this happened'. Can identify past experiences through choice of photo, etc.
Able to place self in future	Shows an ability to think forward (e.g. when we go there we will, next time, soon, in x days, etc.)

Complex information about self (What kind of person am I?): Assessment and resources

Assessment is through observation in a range of setting and/or discussion with a person who knows the child or young person well. Interactive play sessions are also useful (i.e. role play, choice-making games and activities). Useful resources include:

- emotions photos, cards, symbols, books, CD games, etc.
- range of toys, food and activities for choice making
- 'All about me' books, photo albums (past experiences and friends and family) social stories, comic strips, etc.

continued

ELEMENT: SOCIAL SELF (me and others)

Key Skills	Example: How would s/he show this?
Shows an interest in others	Watches, approaches, smiles, etc.
Shows tolerance of others	Will work or play alongside others (even if not interacting)
Establishes shared attention	Demonstrates an ability to share interests with others with a shared experience (e.g. book) (see Flexibility Assessment – Play and Social Development items 6 and 7)
Demonstrates sharing (with adult and/or child)	Able to share a toy/item (e.g. sharing a packet of crisps, sharing building blocks or trains, etc.)
Follows social cues and direction (from adult and/or child)	Acts from a social cue (i.e. will follow a point or gesture, will follow a person or group action) (e.g. lining up, going out to play, etc.)
Demonstrates imitation of others (adults and/or peers)	Will copy a physical action or verbal action
Responds appropriately to others (adults and/or peers)	Response to another's interaction is appropriate to the situation (e.g. greeting, departure, moves away, moves closer as situation requires, etc.)
Approaches others (adult or peer) for interaction help/comfort, etc.	As stated
Adapts behaviour to different people or situations	Shows an awareness that you may behave differently according to people's status (i.e. parent, friend or teacher) or to situation (e.g. school, home, church, etc.) and adapts behaviour accordingly (See Flexibility Assessment – Adaptability)
Demonstrates empathy (towards adults or peers)	Shows an understanding and ability to recognise another's needs and feelings (e.g. will offer comfort, sympathy, knows how they feel and acts accordingly).

Social self (me and others): Assessment and resources

Assessment is through observation in a range of setting and/or discussion with person who knows the child or young person well. As this section relies largely on observing interaction in different contexts, few resources are needed other than the following:

- interactive play sessions are useful (i.e. role play, copying games, Simon says, etc.)
- a range of toys and activities for sharing.

ELEMENT: SELF AS A LEARNER (Me as a learner)

Key Skills	Example: How would s/he show this?
Identifies preferences for social/play activities – behavioural	Will gravitate towards preferred activities or refuse non-preferred (i.e. shows preferences through behaviour)
Identifies preferences for social/play activities – makes a choice	Will make a choice of preferred activities when presented with options – through verbal, sign or symbol
Identifies preferences for learning – behavioural	Will gravitate towards preferred learning style or content or refuse non preferred (i.e. shows preferences through behaviour)
Identifies preferences for learning – makes a choice	Will make a choice of preferred learning style or content when presented with options – through verbal, sign or symbol
Recognises role as a learner	Shows an understanding of and follows routine and structure of lesson (with visual support if needed)
Identifies need for help	Indicates a need for help – behaviourally (i.e. signs of anxiety)
Asks for help	As stated. Communicates verbally, through sign or symbol
Accepts help/direction	As stated. Accepts and responds to help offered
Shows organisation/independence skills (in learning)	Will organise equipment for a task, can start an activity and work through it with independence (according to level of ability)
Shows organisation/independence skills (personal)	Will organise personal possessions, can get ready for school, etc.

Self as a learner (me as a learner): Assessment and resources

As this section relies largely on observing behaviour in different contexts, few resources are needed. Assessment is therefore primarily through observation in a range of setting and/or discussion with person who knows the child or young person well. Resources include:

- selection of learning based activities for choice making
- choice cards/photos depicting different activities/resources available.

continued

ELEMENT: SELF-EVALUATION AND SELF-REFLECTION (How do I do?)

Key Skills	Example: How would s/he show this?
Identifies skills achieved	Identifies skills thorough verbal means, sign or symbol (e.g. I can…). This can be made through choice of symbols/photos, etc. if needed
Identifies strengths (I am good at)	Identifies skills thorough verbal means, sign or symbol (e.g. I am good at…). This can be made through choice of symbols/photos, etc. if needed
Identifies difficulties/weaknesses (I can't – I need help with)	Identifies skills thorough verbal means, sign or symbol (e.g. I need help with, I can't…). This can be made through choice of symbols/photos, etc. if needed
Evaluates level of success – learning (rating)	Is able to (correctly!) rate success through verbal means, sign or symbol (e.g. thumbs up, down or sideways, rating 1–5, colours)
Evaluates level of success – behaviour (rating)	Is able to (correctly!) rate success through verbal means, sign or symbol (e.g. thumbs up, down or sideways, rating 1–5, colours)
Makes suggestions for improvement (targets, goals) – learning	As stated. Using verbal means, sign or symbol. Through choice is needed
Makes suggestions for improvement (targets, goals) – behaviour	As stated. Using verbal means, sign or symbol. Through choice is needed
Recognises and analyses mistakes – learning	As stated. Using verbal means, sign or symbol. Through choice is needed
Recognises and analyses mistakes – behaviour	As stated. Using verbal means, sign or symbol. Through choice is needed

Self-evaluation and self-reflection (How do I do?): Assessment and resources

Assessment is primarily through observation in a range of setting and/or discussion with person who knows the child or young person well. Resources include:

- social stories and comic strips and 'me' mind map formats
- photos and symbols of school based and social activities
- scenarios and what happens next games
- behaviour and learning scales and charts.

Table 6.3 Self-knowledge Assessment Yearly Summary

Name: DoB: Class/group:

Timescale →	A		B		C		D		E	
	Self-definition/self-awareness (What am I like?)		Complex information about self (What kind of person am I?)		Social self (Me and others)		Self as a learner (Me as a learner)		Self-evaluation and self-reflection (How do I do?)	
	Raw Score /30	Percentage	Raw Score /50	Percentage	Raw Score /50	Percentage	Raw Score /50	Percentage	Raw Score /45	Percentage
Baseline										
Term One										
Term Two										
Term Three										

	Baseline	Term One	Term Two	Term Three
Date completed:				
Completed by:				

Table 6.4 Self-knowledge Assessment Yearly Summary Example

Name: xxxxxxxx   DoB: xx/xx/xx   Class/group: 1234

Timescale	A Self-definition/ self-awareness (What am I like?)		B Complex information about self (What kind of person am I?)		C Social self (Me and others)		D Self as a learner (Me as a learner)		E Self-evaluation and self-reflection (How do I do?)	
	Raw Score /30	Percentage	Raw Score /50	Percentage	Raw Score /50	Percentage	Raw Score /50	Percentage	Raw Score /45	Percentage
Baseline	10	33	11	22	9	18	9	18	9	20
Term One	13	43	13	26	13	26	13	26	9	20
Term Two	19	63	15	30	18	36	13	26	9	20
Term Three	21	70	17	34	20	40	14	28	9	20

Baseline	Term One	Term Two	Term Three

Date completed:

Completed by:

Table 6.5 Self-knowledge Quick Reference Summary Chart

(A) Self-definition/physical self

Item	Scale
Shows awareness of physical and sensory needs	1 2 3 4 5
Gives behavioural expression of feelings/emotions	1 2 3 4 5
Recognises own actions on environment. Cause and effect	1 2 3 4 5
Demonstrates early self-definition (recognising self, name, possessions)	1 2 3 4 5
Shows developing self-recognition (basic information about self – hair, colour, all about me)	1 2 3 4 5
Recognises own actions on people (e.g. smiles, hugs)	1 2 3 4 5

Key:
1 = Not present
2 = Emerging
3 = Developing new abilities
4 = Using new abilities
5 = Established

(B) Complex information about self

Item	Scale
Identifies preferences (likes and dislikes)	1 2 3 4 5
Identifies dislikes	1 2 3 4 5
Identifies own feelings (recognition)	1 2 3 4 5
Understands reasons for feelings (understanding)	1 2 3 4 5
Recognises consequences of own actions/behaviour	1 2 3 4 5
Identifies personality traits/personal qualities	1 2 3 4 5
Demonstrates self-interest (uses 'I')	1 2 3 4 5
Recognises differences to others (I like/she likes)	1 2 3 4 5
Able to place self in past	1 2 3 4 5
Able to place self in future	1 2 3 4 5

(C) Social self (self in social situations)

Item	Scale
Shows interest in others	1 2 3 4 5
Shows tolerance of others	1 2 3 4 5
Establishes shared attention	1 2 3 4 5
Demonstrates sharing (with adult and child)	1 2 3 4 5
Follows social cues and direction (from adult and child)	1 2 3 4 5
Demonstrates imitation of others (adult and peers)	1 2 3 4 5
Responds appropriately to others (adult and peers)	1 2 3 4 5
Approaches others for interaction/help/comfort	1 2 3 4 5
Adapts response to different people/situations	1 2 3 4 5
Demonstrates empathy	1 2 3 4 5

(D) Self as a learner

Item	Scale
Identifies preferences for activities – behavioural	1 2 3 4 5
Identifies preferences for activities – makes a choice	1 2 3 4 5
Identifies preferences for learning – behavioural	1 2 3 4 5
Identifies preferences for learning – makes a choice	1 2 3 4 5
Recognises role as a learner (i.e. understands and follows routine and structure of lesson)	1 2 3 4 5
Identifies need for help	1 2 3 4 5
Asks for help	1 2 3 4 5
Accepts help/direction	1 2 3 4 5
Shows organisation/independence skills (in learning)	1 2 3 4 5
Shows organisation/independence skills (personal)	1 2 3 4 5

(E) Self-evaluation and self-reflection

Item	Scale
Identifies skills	1 2 3 4 5
Identifies strengths	1 2 3 4 5
Identifies difficulties/weaknesses	1 2 3 4 5
Evaluates success – learning	1 2 3 4 5
Evaluates success – behaviour	1 2 3 4 5
Makes suggestions for improvement – learning	1 2 3 4 5
Makes suggestions for improvement – behaviour	1 2 3 4 5
Recognises and analyses mistakes – learning	1 2 3 4 5
Recognises and analyses mistakes – behaviour	1 2 3 4 5

continued

SCORING

A Self-definition/ physical self

Timescale	Raw Score
Baseline	
Term 1	
Term 2	
Term 3	

B Complex information about self

Timescale	Raw Score
Baseline	
Term 1	
Term 2	
Term 3	

C Social self (self in social situations)

Timescale	Raw Score
Baseline	
Term 1	
Term 2	
Term 3	

D Self as a learner

Timescale	Raw Score
Baseline	
Term 1	
Term 2	
Term 3	

E Self-evaluation and self-reflection

Timescale	Raw Score
Baseline	
Term 1	
Term 2	
Term 3	

Identifying priorities and setting targets

As identified above, the 5P Approach Self-knowledge Assessment contains a number of statements all representing self-knowledge skills within five areas which broadly follow a developmental pattern. Statements within each area (A, B, C, D or E) also follow a broadly developmental pattern (recorded from top to bottom on the checklists). Priorities for intervention should therefore usually be taken from the first areas on the continuum i.e. A – B – C, etc. and/or from the first statements within these areas. Priorities for intervention are therefore identified on the following basis:

- Those skills or gaps identified within areas where other skills have been achieved.

- Those skills which represent the next developmental stage.

- Those skills which present a major challenge in terms of barriers to learning, well-being or behaviour.

- Those skills which are easiest to address/plan for.

Teaching and developing new skills

Once priority areas have been identified and targets set, the Assessment and Resources section found within the Recording Self-knowledge Observations and Skill Achievement (Table 6.2) can be used to provide activities designed specifically to develop identified skills. Using a project format in a folder or photo album or scrap book labelled 'About Me', new information learned can be stored and revisited again and again and forms the basis of discussions.

There are numerous resources available on the market to support the development of self-knowledge and to support the individual to develop a view of themselves as a person. This includes some materials specifically designed to look at different aspects of disability and disorder. These can be used selectively to address key areas identified for development. However, as with the development of flexibility skills, it is important that any skills learned are not learned solely in one context but are generalised into everyday life and put into functional use as much as possible. Use of real life situations, photos, video and such like will aid this.

Self-expression – the third area of the participation triad

For the purpose of enabling participation, communication and self-expression is defined as the ability to understand information given, to understand what is expected of this and the ability to express a view. In addition to the expressive and receptive language skills needed to express a view, this also requires the ability to think, plan, do and review, very closely linked to the development of self-knowledge and flexibility of thought. Although to those without difficulties in this area, giving an opinion when asked appears relatively easy, this is a very complex process. In simple terms this means understanding the question, working out what is required, reflecting on information about yourself, relating this to what is required, forming an opinion, forming an answer, planning and sequencing a response – lots of steps and stages for those with flexibility issues!

In other words simply having the means to understand what is asked and a way of communicating your views, whether this be by verbal means, signs, pictures or symbols, does not enable you to express a view. For this you need to understand yourself, your likes, dislikes, needs and then to be able to follow through a process of actively (or functionally) using those communication, problem-solving and self-knowledge skills to form a view or give an opinion. To develop participation skills and to inform those supporting individuals with special needs, it is important to distinguish between the independent expression of views, a responsive expression of views and a passive expression of views as these represent stages along a participation continuum.

Independent expression of views

In addition to the development of flexibility and self-knowledge skills as outlined above, expressing a view independently, without prompt, requires the development of *functional* communication skills: the ability to communicate to others for a purpose (and to identify the need to do this). Functional communication is *active*. It is initiated by the individual without prompt and is spontaneous. Self-expression (expressing a view) therefore, in addition to having a means to communicate, requires an understanding of the purpose of communication, a degree of flexibility and adaptability, and the ability to understand oneself and others.

The development of active or functional communication skills provides the individual with a means of influencing their immediate environment and the ability to independently give information to others on their thoughts, feelings and views. Frost and Bondy (1994) and Bondy (1996) identify key areas of early functional communication, splitting skills into those that are 'critical' and those that are 'useful'. Critical skills would include requesting and rejecting and affirming or agreeing, whereas useful skills would include the ability to comment or greet and so on.

This is a very useful distinction and allows those supporting the individual with functional communication difficulty to identify and prioritise areas for intervention and support. Developing these functional communication skills is a crucial first step in developing an ability to express a view and self-advocate.

Responsive expression of views

In many situations, however, children and young people are encouraged to make verbal or non-verbal responses to adult initiated questions. Although the child or young person may not have developed or may not use the ability to spontaneously or actively communicate needs, preferences or feelings, she or he may give a response to an adult initiated interaction or question whether the response is through verbal means, sign, symbol, choice of pictures, sentences and so forth.

Noting a child or young person's response to a particular question may give information more reliably than simple interpretation, but there are also issues to consider. Many situations arise in school where questions are posed to elicit a view or response from a child or young person, but it is important to recognise that they will only show a response in relation to the question posed and the choices given. There is no guarantee that the choices made accurately reflect their view or that this view is based on a real understanding of themselves and their needs (i.e. accurate self-knowledge). This has implications for those who set about eliciting the views of children and young people, and it is important to avoid situations where they are presented with limited information or limited choices and where this is the only information used to ascertain a view.

As we have seen from the information above, responding to a question posed in a particular way and using materials already provided are very different skills from spontaneously expressing a view (or being able to think, plan and do without support). Nonetheless, despite reservations, this provides a valuable means of eliciting views from those individuals who have not yet developed the skills they need to do this independently.

Passive expression of views

Where the child or young person has not yet developed the skills they need to communicate their views spontaneously or to respond to questions (however posed), their needs, feelings and views may be interpreted by others observing their behaviour and drawing conclusions about their views from this information; for example observing preference for certain toys or foods (a passive expression of views) or making a judgement about whether they are happy and content in a situation.

However, a reliance on others interpreting behaviour can lead to frequent misinterpretations. When observing behaviour it is easy to make false assumptions. There is a danger that behaviour is interpreted according to the observer's views and preferences rather than being a true reflection of that person's views. This is known as Attribution Theory, where a person may *attribute* a meaning to an other's behaviour according to their own beliefs about that person or to the context at the time.

It is important therefore to base judgements of this type on evidence from a variety of sources and situations and on detailed knowledge of how the individual shows their views and feelings. An evidence-based observation record, Showing Views and Feelings, which has been designed specifically for use with children and young people who are at this stage of development, can be found in Table 6.6.

A blank copy can be found in Table 6.7. This observation record can be used to provide evidence based information upon which to form a judgement about an individual's views on something when they do not have the self-expression or self-awareness skills to respond in any other way.

Expressing views – a developmental progression

There are many opportunities within both home and school when children and young people may be invited to express a view and participate in day to day activities on an informal basis. In the school setting, most *statutory* (legal) educational requirements for eliciting the views of pupils however focus largely on complex information such as taking part in evaluating progress and giving views on school provision and placement. There are equally complex questions posed to the individual within the care setting. It is generally recognised, however, that each individual would participate at a level appropriate to their development and skills. This leads us to assume that there must be a developmental progression in ability to express views, beginning with the least complex stages (this links back to the concept of a participation continuum).

In addition to the development of functional and expressive skills outlined above, the ability to participate and express a view or opinion also requires an understanding of vocabulary about oneself and of increasingly complex concepts. Initially this may be general vocabulary and 'labels', extending to attributes such as size and colour and then to more complex and abstract concepts such as like and dislike and feelings and emotions.

Table 6.6 Showing Views and Feelings Observation Record Example

How does… show:	Verbal means	Non-verbal means: behaviour	Non-verbal means: expression/body language/sign or symbol	Example: How does s/he show this?	Observed by:
Preferences	Says: 'I want' 'I like', etc.	Seeks out item Makes a choice, etc.	Smiles/laughs, etc.	Provide specific and concrete example of how and when this occurs based on several observations. Support with photo or video as appropriate and cross reference to this source	
Dislikes	Says: 'I don't want' 'I hate', etc.	Rejects/Pushes away Makes a choice, etc.	Scowls, cries, etc.		
Agreement (consent)	Says: 'Yes' 'OK' 'I want', 'More', etc.	Makes choice Participates Approaches	Smiles Nods Signs		
Disagreement (withholding consent)	Says: 'no' 'go away' 'stop', etc.	Moves away Hits Withdraws	Grimaces Shakes head		
Happiness/ contentment	Says: 'happy', etc.	Claps hands, flaps, etc.	Smiles/laughs, etc.		
Sadness/ discontent	Says 'sad', etc.	Hits self Drops to the floor, etc.	Expression		
Anxiety/fear	Says: 'help', 'stop' 'frightened', etc.	Hurts self (bangs head) Runs out of room Hides under table Hits out	Grimaces Cries, moans		
Anger	Says: 'no' 'stop' 'Go away', etc.	Spits Stamps Kicks or hits anyone or thing nearby	Screams loudly Makes fists Body tenses		

Table 6.7 Showing Views and Feelings Observation Record

Name: Date completed: Completed by:

How does… show:	Verbal means	Non-verbal means: behaviour	Non-verbal means: expression/body language/sign or symbol	Example: How does s/he show this?	Observed by:
Preferences					
Dislikes					
Agreement (consent)					
Disagreement (withholding consent)					
Happiness/ contentment					
Sadness/discontent					
Anxiety/fear					
Anger					

The SP Approach

As we can see from the earlier part of this chapter, the development of these later concepts also requires the development of self-knowledge and skills in self-evaluation and in flexible thinking, all of which overlap and interrelate.

Developing an ability to express a view therefore requires:

- expressive and receptive skills and vocabulary

- functional (active) communication skills, motivation

- flexible thinking and adaptability

- knowledge about complex and abstract concepts

- self-knowledge

- adaptability and flexibility and the ability to generalise and use knowledge and skills.

It appears therefore that there is also a developmental continuum for the ability to express views (self-expression) which differs from the developmental pathways of expressive and receptive language skills and functional communication skills. A suggested model looking specifically at those self-expression skills which are linked to participation and flexibility is presented within the 5P Approach Expressing Views Assessment.

The 5P Approach Expressing Views Assessment

As we have seen, the ability to express a view is crucial to the development of independence and is a key factor in an individual's level of participation within school and community. It is also crucial to their degree of self-advocacy. In order to express a view, an individual requires not only the necessary vocabulary and expressive and receptive language skills but also the ability to use these skills functionally in a variety of contexts (linked to flexibility). In order to express a view about your thoughts and feelings and to give an opinion or make a decision, you first need to understand yourself as a person (self-knowledge). This assessment has been designed therefore to complement the 5P Approach Self-knowledge Assessment and the 5P Approach Flexibility Assessment.

As with the other 5P Approach assessments contained within this book, the 5P Approach Expressing Views Assessment provides a basis for a formative and summative assessment of self-expression skills. Areas chosen follow a developmental scale or continuum and focus specifically on areas which relate to self-knowledge, flexible thinking and independence.

The structure of the 5P Approach Expressing Views Assessment is similar to that of the 5P Approach Flexibility Assessment and the 5P Approach Assessment of Self-knowledge. The level of skill development within each distinct element of the assessment is graded from 1: not present to 5: established and the Scoring Key is also the same as in the other two assessments (see Table 3.2).

This assessment therefore provides a means of identifying targets and monitoring progress within a specific area which is often not included within traditional curriculum-based assessments and links with national agendas such as Pupil Participation and Pupil Voice (DfES 2004c), Citizenship and the Assessment for Learning Strategy (DCSF 2008).

The 5P Approach Expressing Views Assessment comprises:

- the Expressing Views Continuum

- the Expressing Views Checklist

- the Expressing Views Assessment Summary.

The Expressing Views Continuum

Linking closely with the 5P Approach Self-knowledge Assessment, this continuum has been constructed to broadly follow a developmental progression of self-expression from the early stages of the functional use of communication to request and to reject, to the more complex process of talking about thoughts and feelings, opinions and so on.

The continuum identifies skill areas which follow this developmental pathway and which are broken down into five overall categories: A: Early Skills – making a request, B: Early Skills – rejecting, C: Early Skills – making a choice, D: Later Skills and E: Skills related specifically to self-knowledge. Each of these categories is further broken down into key skills. The Expressing Views Continuum can be found in Table 6.8.

Table 6.8 The Expressing Views Continuum

Early Skills A, B, C			Later Skills D					
To request	To reject	To make a choice	To comment	To describe (concrete, simple attributes)	To question	To describe (complex attributes, abstract)	To reason/explain (cause and effect)	To predict, plan and imagine
Skills relating to			Self-knowledge E					
Showing a preference non-verbally and through behaviour	Expressing feelings non-verbally/behaviourally	Showing (recognition of) feelings (simple), agreement and disagreement	Giving personal traits (simple)	Talking about events (recalling activities in relation to self)	Self-evaluation – skills (simple)	Self-evaluation – skills (complex)	Self-evaluation – behaviour (complex)	Making suggestions for improvement
Showing a preference verbally (I want, I like, etc.)			Giving personal information (family/friends, etc.)	Talking about feelings verbally (complex)	Self-evaluation – behaviour (simple)		Self-evaluation – skills (complex)	
				Talking about beliefs and thoughts				

The Expressing Views Checklist

This checklist uses the same overall format as the other 5P Approach assessments found within this book and can be found in Table 6.9.

Using the elements of the Expressing Views Continuum as its basis, this checklist identifies key skills within each category, each scored separately. The first step is to provide a baseline (B). Each element comprises several statements describing behaviour indicating a self-expression skill. Each statement is given a score of 1–5 (not present – established) in the assessed level of achievement column according to the level of skill development to date. When scoring skill areas, *all* developmental statements must be scored. If skills are already present these are scored at 5 (according to the level of skill development to date).

Scores given are based on observation and the subjective judgement of those who know the child/young person best. Qualitative information recording 'how does s/he show this?' is also recorded on the sheet for each statement. This checklist also has further capacity to record the type and style of communication: verbal, non-verbal, active, passive and so on. Further detail on this can be found on the first page of the 5P Approach Expressing Views Checklist along with a key to notation used.

These columns have been included within the checklist in order to record skills as they emerge and to acknowledge an individual's skills and method of self-expression. The focus of this particular assessment is to look at self-expression skills whatever the form regardless of an individual's verbal language ability. For example, a score of 5 can be given if an individual is able to express a view to meet biological needs using visual symbols (as this is a self-expression skill) even though other learning based targets may have identified increasing verbal expressive vocabulary.

A total for each category is calculated and recorded at the bottom of the page. In order to monitor progress, the checklist has the capacity for baseline and termly assessment (record in B, T1, T2, T3). These totals are then recorded on the Expressing Views Assessment Summary.

As with the development of self-knowledge, individuals with social communication difficulties may display skills out of developmental sequence. This checklist and assessment summary therefore has the capacity to identify specific skill achievement and also any gaps which may require intervention.

Table 6.9 The Expressing Views Checklist

How to use this checklist

The checklist comprises five categories:

A. Early skills – making a request

B. Early skills – rejecting

C. Early skills – making a choice

D. Later skills

E. Skills relating to self-knowledge.

Each is scored separately. The first step is to provide a baseline. Each category comprises several statements describing behaviour which indicates a self-expression skill. Each item is given a score (in the assessed level column T1) according to the level of skill development to date.

Description	Score
Not present	1
Emerging	2
Developing new skills	3
Using new skills	4
Established	5

Scores given are based on observation and the subjective judgement of those who know the child/young person best. Qualitative information recording 'how does s/he show this?' is also recorded on the sheet for each skill when a score of 5 is achieved. A sub-total for each category is calculated and recorded at the bottom of the column and, where required, brought forward to the top of the next page. These totals are then recorded on the Expressing Views Assessment Yearly Summary to provide a quick reference skill overview.

Recording the type of communication

Individuals may express a view verbally or non-verbally, actively or passively (i.e. someone observes and interprets). This checklist therefore also has capacity for recording the mode (type of communication) and the means (active or passive) of communication and can be used not only as a measure of progress through skill acquisition but also to identify next steps in supporting individuals towards independence. The recording key is set out below.

Recording Key

WHAT? The area of self-expression	WHY? The purpose of communication	Assessed Level of Achievement Place on scale of 1–5 1= Not Present 2= Emerging 3= Developing new skills 4= Using new skills 5= Established	WITH? (Mode/type of communication) N = Non-verbal (behaviour) A = Augmentative (sign, symbol, picture) V = Verbal	HOW? (Style) P = Passive (observed – no communication with other) R = Responsive (responds to offer, request, etc.) A = Active (seeks out other to communicate)	Example: How does s/he show this? Please include: • frequency • degree of generalisation • no of items • range of people

Copyright © Linda Miller 2013

The 5P Approach Expressing Views Checklist   EARLY SKILLS: A

WHAT?	WHY?	Assessed Level				WITH? N/A/V	HOW? P/R/A	Example: How does s/he show this?	Person contributing to assessment
		B	T1	T2	T3				
Making a request	To meet biological needs (e.g. food, drink, toilet)								
	To meet self-care needs (e.g. clothing, coat on/off, wash hands, etc.)								
	To meet social needs (e.g. physical contact, interaction/play) (with person)								
	To meet leisure needs (e.g. play objects/activities)								
	To meet learning needs (e.g. learning activities, apparatus/tools)								
TOTAL		—25	—25	—25	—25				

The 5P Approach Expressing Views Checklist EARLY SKILLS: B

WHAT?	WHY?	Assessed Level				WITH? N/A/V	HOW? P/R/A	Example: How does s/he show this?	Person contributing to assessment
		B	T1	T2	T3				
To reject	To meet biological needs (e.g. food, drink, toilet)								
	To meet self-care needs (e.g. clothing, coat on/off, wash hands, etc.)								
	To meet social needs (e.g. physical contact, interaction/ play) (with person)								
	To meet leisure needs (e.g. play objects/activities)								
	To meet learning needs (e.g. learning activities, apparatus/ tools)								
	TOTAL	$\frac{}{25}$	$\frac{}{25}$	$\frac{}{25}$	$\frac{}{25}$				

continued

The 5P Approach Expressing Views Checklist   EARLY SKILLS: C

WHAT?	WHY?	Assessed Level				WITH? N/A/V	HOW? P/R/A	Example: How does s/he show this?	Person contributing to assessment
		B	T1	T2	T3				
To make a choice from	**Biological/self-care (e.g. food/drink/clothes)**	B	T1	T2	T3				
	1 preferred/1 non-preferred								
	Small selection of preferred/non-preferred								
	Small selection of preferred								
	Large selection of preferred								
	Social (e.g. interaction/play objects)	B	T1	T2	T3				
	1 preferred/1 non-preferred								
	Small selection of preferred/non-preferred								
	Small selection of preferred								
	Large selection of preferred								
	Learning (e.g. activities/materials)	B	T1	T2	T3				
	1 preferred/1 non-preferred								
	Small selection of preferred/non-preferred								
	Small selection of preferred								
	Large selection of preferred								
	TOTAL	— 60	— 60	— 60					

The 5P Approach Expressing Views Checklist   LATER SKILLS: D

WHAT? WHEN?	Assessed Level				WITH? N/A/V	HOW? P/R/A	Examples:	Person contributing to assessment
	B	T1	T2	T3				
In social situations								
Describe (concrete facts, simple events, etc.)								
Question (why did that happen? What are we going to do?, etc.)								
Describe (complex/abstract situations or events)								
Reason/explain (cause and effect): 'this happened because.'								
Predict, plan and imagine: 'if we do this, this will happen, etc.'								
In learning situations	B	T1	T2	T3				
Making a comment								
Describing (concrete, simple information and attributes)								
Question (why did that happen? What will he do next?, etc.)								
Describe (complex/abstract information and attributes)								
Reason/explain (cause and effect): 'this happens because....'								
Predict, plan and imagine: 'if we do this, this will happen', etc.)								
TOTAL	55	55	55	55				

continued

The 5P Approach

The 5P Approach Expressing Views Checklist   RELATING TO SELF-KNOWLEDGE: E

WHAT? WHY?	Assessed Level			WITH? N/A/V	HOW? P/R/A	Examples:	Person contributing to assessment
	B	T1	T2	T3			
Expressing preference non-verbally/behaviourally							
Expressing preferences verbally (I want, don't want, etc.)							
Giving a view, simple (I like, don't like, etc.)							
Expressing feelings non-verbally/behaviourally							
Communicating (recognition of) feelings, simple (I am happy/sad, etc.)							
Describing personal traits (physical, simple)							
Relaying personal information (my family/friends, etc.)							
Describing events, recalling activities (in relation to self)							
Giving views about people (my friend is, etc.)							
Expressing feelings verbally (complex)							
SUB-TOTAL							

The 5P Approach Expressing Views Checklist   RELATING TO SELF-KNOWLEDGE: E

WHAT? WHY?	Assessed Level				WITH? N/A/V	HOW? P/R/A	Examples:	Person contributing to assessment
	B	T1	T2	T3				
SUB-TOTAL CARRIED FORWARD								
Expressing beliefs and thoughts (I think that…)								
Self-evaluation – skills, simple (I can, can't, etc.)								
Asks for help								
Describing personal traits, complex (what kind of person I am)								
Self-evaluation – behaviour, simple (describe)								
Self-evaluation – skills, complex (reason, explain)								
Suggestions for improvement (predict, plan and imagine)								
TOTAL	85	85	85	85				

The Expressing Views Yearly Summary

As with the other 5P Approach assessments, this provides a visual summative profile for the individual, mapping the acquisition of self-expression skills and plotting progress. It provides a means of identifying overall totals within each category of the Expressing Views Continuum and is constructed to provide a means of measuring and recording progress from a baseline on a termly basis. The numerical and percentage scoring system used provides a means of measuring small step progress within each area. The numerical scores can also be placed into a database to plot progress over a greater length of time and to allow comparison of degree of progress across individuals or across groups (see Table 6.10).

Identifying priorities and setting targets

As identified above, the 5P Approach Expressing Views Assessment contains a number of statements all representing self-expression skills within five areas which broadly follow a developmental pattern. Statements within each area (A, B, C, D or E) also follow a broadly developmental pattern (recorded from top to bottom on the checklists). Priorities for intervention should therefore usually be taken from the first areas on the continuum (i.e. A – B – C, etc.) and/or from the first statements within these areas. Priorities for intervention are therefore identified on the following basis:

- those skills or gaps identified within areas where other skills have been achieved

- those skills which represent a move towards independence (i.e. a change of style or mode of communication)

- those skills which represent the next developmental stage

- those skills which present a major challenge in terms of barriers to learning, well-being or behaviour

- those which are easiest to address/plan for.

As discussed earlier in this section, this assessment tool is designed specifically with the development of self-expression as part of three key skills which enable participation and the development of independence. The priority is therefore equipping the individual with a means of expressing a view whether that is verbally or non-verbally. The focus for development may well be different from the focus of a language or communication target which might have other priorities.

The focus for supporting the development of self-expression is moving towards independence. When looking at next steps therefore, this may be a change in the type or style of communication (i.e. using an active or functional form of communication as opposed to a current responsive style) rather than moving onto a next level of development.

Table 6.10 The Expressing Views Yearly Summary

Name: DoB: Class/group:

Timescale	A Early skills: making a request		B Early skills: to reject		C Early skills: to make a choice		D Later skills		E Skills related to self-knowledge	
	Raw Score /25	Percentage	Raw Score /25	Percentage	Raw Score /60	Percentage	Raw Score /55	Percentage	Raw Score /85	Percentage
Baseline										
Term One										
Term Two										
Term Three										

	Baseline	Term One	Term Two	Term Three

Date completed:

Completed by:

Teaching and developing new skills

Once priority areas have been identified and targets set, the next step is to support the development of new self-expression skills. As this area is so closely interrelated with the development of self-knowledge and flexibility skills (and also the development of wider expressive and receptive language and functional communication skills), the best way to set about developing these skills is through functional and practical activities and alongside the flexibility and self-knowledge skill development. Suggested activities which encourage the development and use of these skills can be found in the next chapter. As with the development of self-knowledge, using a project format in a folder or photo album or book such as an About Me book, new information learned can be stored and revisited again and again and forms the basis of discussions.

As for self-knowledge, there are numerous resources available on the market to support the development of these skills and to support the individual to develop and express a view of themselves as a person and relay personal information. Resources aimed at developing self-esteem are particularly useful as they begin with understanding yourself and your qualities and strengths. Examples include *Helping Children to Build Self-esteem* (Plummer and Harper 2001), *101 Games for Self-esteem* (Mosley et al. 2002) and *Self-esteem Games* (Sher 1998). Publishers of educational games such as Winslow Press and Pearson Education have a range of practical activities and games. Again, these resources can be used selectively to address key areas identified for development. However, as with the development of self-knowledge and flexibility skills, it is important that any skills learned are not learned solely in one context but are generalised into everyday life and put into functional use as much as possible. Use of real life situations, photos, video and other media will aid this.

Where next?

This chapter has explored the relationship between flexibility and participation or pupil voice and has identified flexibility as one of the three key interrelating skills (the participation triad) an individual needs to overcome the barriers to participation related to their condition:

1. *Involvement* – the skills, understanding and motivation to become involved in decision-making processes (adaptability), the ability to apply and generalise skills for differing purposes (flexibility).

2. *Self-awareness* – the ability to understand and identify needs and to self-evaluate (to understand yourself and others).

3. *Communication and self-expression* – the ability to understand information given, what is expected and the ability to express a view (in addition to the language skills needed, this requires the ability to think, plan, do and review).

Flexibility in particular holds the key as the ability to think flexibly, to use skills functionally and to adapt to the circumstances which arise is the mechanism which brings together and organises the skills and information we need to reflect, make an informed choice and to express our views and to participate actively. Developing flexibility skills should therefore be the main focus of any policy and practice designed to enable the participation of children and young people with social communication difficulty and likewise to enable participation or pupil voice to be included as a key element of any flexibility policy and curriculum.

The assessments outlined in this chapter can be used in conjunction with the 5P Approach Flexibility Assessment introduced in Chapter 2 to identify areas of strength and areas for future development. Looking at the baseline skills already achieved, this information can be used to inform the type of resources, materials and environment the individual currently needs to reduce stress and anxiety, to break down the barriers to learning and to maximise their potential to make progress (i.e. creating a GREEN Zone).

However, as we see in Chapter 4, creating a GREEN Zone is just the first step. The next step is to move forward along the Flexibility Continuum and further towards independence, expanding the GREEN Zone along the way! This is done by developing flexibility-specific skills and by providing opportunities to use the skills which are developing and have developed.

The next chapter looks at how this can be brought together within a flexibility policy and a flexibility curriculum.

References

Alderson, P. and Montgomery, J. (1996) *Health Care Choices: Making Decisions with Children.* London: Institute for Public Policy Research.

Baron-Cohen, S. (1997) *Mindblindness: An Essay on Autism and Theory of Mind.* Cambridge, MA: Bradford Books, MIT Press. (external).

Bondy, A.S. (1996) *The Pyramid Approach to Education, 1st edition.* Newark, DE: Pyramid Educational Consultants, Inc.

The Children Act (1989) London: HMSO.

Damon, W. and Hart, D. (1991) *Self Understanding in Childhood and Adolescence.* Cambridge Studies in Social Development, Issue 7. Cambridge: Cambridge University Press.

Department for Children, Schools and Families (DCSF) (2008) *The Assessment for Learning Strategy.* Crown Copyright. London: DCSF.

Department for Education and Skills (DfES) (2001) *Revised Code of Practice for Special Educational Needs.* London: DfES.

Department for Education and Skills (DfES) (2004a) *Every Child Matters: Change for Children.* Crown Copyright. London: DfES.

Department for Education and Skills (DfES) (2004b) *Removing Barriers to Achievement – The Government's Strategy for SEN.* SEN Update 14. Crown Copyright. London: DfES.

Department for Education and Skills (DfES) (2004c) *Working Together: Giving Children and Young People a Say.* London: DfES.

Department for Education and Skills (DfES) and Department of Health (DoH) (2002) *Autistic Spectrum Disorders: Good Practice Guidance.* Crown Copyright. London: DfES.

Frost, L. and Bondy, A. (1994). *The Picture Exchange Communication System (PECS) Training Manual.* Newark, DE: Pyramid Educational Consultants, Inc.

Gersch, I.S. (1987) 'Involving Pupils in their Own Assessment.' In T. Bowers (ed.) *Special Educational Needs and Human Resource Management.* London: Croom Helm.

Human Rights Act (1998) London: HMSO (in force in UK, October 2000).

Mosley, J., Sonnet, H., Cripps, M. and Hoskin, B. (2002) *101 Games for Self-esteem.* Oxford: Blackwell.

Neisser, U. (1997) 'The Roots of Self-knowledge: Perceiving Self, It, and Thou.' In J.G. Snodgrass and R.L. Thompson (eds) *The Self Across Psychology: Self-recognition, Self-awareness, and the Self-concept.* New York: New York Academy of Sciences.

Plummer, D.M. and Harper A.H. (2001) *Helping Children to Build Self-esteem: A Photocopiable Activities Book.* London and Philadelphia: Jessica Kingsley Publishers.

Roller, J. (1998) 'Facilitating pupil involvement in assessment, planning and review processes.' *Educational Psychology in Practice 13*, 4, 226–273.

Sher, B. (1998) *Self-esteem Games.* Oxford: J. Wiley & Sons.

Shier, H. (2001) 'Pathways to participation: openings, opportunities and obligations.' *Children and Society 15*, 107–117.

The Special Educational Needs and Disability Act (2001) London: HMSO.

United Nations (1989) *United Nations Convention on the Rights of the Child* (ratified in UK, December 1999).

Chapter 7

CREATING A FLEXIBILITY POLICY AND FLEXIBILITY CURRICULUM

Why create a flexibility policy and curriculum? As this book demonstrates, the development of flexibility skills is crucial to the development of independence – independence in thinking, in learning and in behaviour. Poor flexibility is also frequently linked to high anxiety and has a significant effect on an individual's well-being and emotional development. Many aspects of the formal and informal teaching and learning of social skills involve the need to develop and apply flexibility skills. As can be seen from the earlier chapters in this book, however, in individuals who present with flexibility difficulties, these skills do not generally develop spontaneously but require some specific, targeted intervention.

Creating a flexibility policy and a flexibility curriculum therefore reflects the importance of addressing flexibility and targets a specific and specialised area not generally included as a separate element within an educational or social curriculum or within schemes of work or care plans.

The 5P Approach to Flexibility set out in Chapter 2 stresses the importance of the four key intervention strands which work together. Just as when working on an individual basis, these strands can be used as a basis for the development of a flexibility policy and curriculum within the whole organisation looking at:

- The general approach – The GREEN zone

- Developing flexibility skills

- Providing opportunity to use flexibility skills

- Teaching and using coping and self-management strategies.

What then should a flexibility policy include?

A. Information about flexibility and why it is important (see Chapter 1).

B. The philosophy, overall approach and environment (the GREEN zone): Flexibility strand one.

C. The curriculum (teaching and developing skills): Flexibility strands two, three and four.

D. Assessment and monitoring of progress (see Chapter 3).

E. Links with other policies.

A. Information about flexibility and why it is important

Information from Chapter 1 can be used for this section to provide an overview of flexibility. It is also important to use concrete examples taken from individuals within the organisation (generalised and not named!) to demonstrate how flexibility strengths and difficulties present and how this affects individuals' access to the opportunities offered.

B. The (organisational) GREEN Zone

This section should include all the *general* strategies, approaches and resources used which create a secure flexibility-friendly environment aimed at reducing stress and meeting the needs of those with flexibility difficulties. The ideas and resources as set out in Chapter 5 can be used as a basis for this. It includes information on supporting transitions, problem solving and adaptability and the overall approach to planning and activities. This section of the flexibility policy would also include any strategies and approaches which have developed as a direct result of successful behaviour intervention (prevention, expanding the GREEN Zone and learning from experience).

As this is a *policy* rather than a personal development plan, the GREEN Zone would include the general approach and philosophy and a broad overview of strategies and activities at an organisational and group (or class) level. This can then be refined according to individual need when individual plans are created (see the Flexibility Strands Planner, Figure 4.2). For those beginning the process of looking at their organisational GREEN Zone, the Flexibility Strands Planner can also be used at the organisational or group level to identify and outline how each of the four strands are being addressed.

C. The Flexibility Curriculum

This section of the policy would include setting out the concept of a Flexibility Continuum, the approach to the teaching and development of flexibility skills and coping or self-management strategies. This also includes the process of identification of areas for development (linked to assessment), target setting and planning and the monitoring of progress.

Guidance and a general overview of what type of teaching approach and environment would meet the needs of individuals placed at Levels One to Five along the Flexibility Continuum is set out in Table 7.1.

Table 7.1 The Flexibility Continuum – Teaching Approaches and Environment Guidance

	LEVEL ONE	LEVEL TWO	LEVEL THREE	LEVEL FOUR	LEVEL FIVE
Teaching Approaches and Environment Guidance	Working with the learning style. Creating a safe, structured environment for the reduction of stress	Teaching and developing coping strategies: A structured approach with some challenge and change and taught opportunity to use coping strategies	Teaching and developing new skills: A structured approach with some challenge and change and opportunity to use newly developing skills	Providing opportunities for generalisation of skills taught and learned: A less structured and predictable approach	Providing opportunities for problem-solving and independence: Minimal structure, maximum opportunity for independent thinking and behaviour
	A highly structured and visually supported environment (pictures or symbols). Clear, and well organised with little change. Use of approaches such as TEACCH. Use of short visual timetables for direction. Activities have clear beginning and end. Minimal change and transition. Rule based and structured approach to teaching and learning	Developing from Level One. Increased *prompted* use of schedules and timetables (towards independence). Opportunities for supported transition and change. Structured timetable and activities including some structured and taught elements of choice and surprise	Developing from Level Two. Independent use of timetables and transition support. Increased presentation of problem-solving opportunities, choice, change and creativity. Slow decrease in use of prompts and increase in use of newly developing skills	Developing from Levels One to Three. Moving towards group timetable/diary system rather than individual. Less structured timetable with increased opportunities for more complex social and learning, problem solving and creativity. Increased opportunities for choice. Independent use of visual support as needed. Increased opportunity for the functional use and generalisation of newly acquired skills	Developing from Levels One to Four. Less specialised and structured timetable and activities. Minimum use of prompts and support (as needed). Increased independence and independent use of acquired skills and self-management strategies

The teaching and development of new skills may involve some specific and discrete teaching of skills (and planned opportunities to generalise and use these functionally) but should also include links with the teaching and learning policy, setting out where flexibility skill teaching fits in with activity planning (as an added layer to curriculum based targets and outcomes). For example, an education based outcome for a maths lesson may place a focus on the development of a mathematical concept whereas the flexibility skill focus for that session could be on developing problem-solving skills or managing within task transitions.

This section of the flexibility policy would also set out what the organisation does to provide opportunities to use flexibility skills. Some suggested ideas and resources linked to providing opportunity to develop flexibility skills are set out in Table 7.2.

Table 7.2 Providing Opportunities to Develop and Use Flexibility Skills
ELEMENT: PLAY AND SOCIAL DEVELOPMENT

Opportunities and activities	Strategies and examples
1. Structured play activities: • Constructive • Symbolic • Creative • Imaginative/role play	Building, construction toys, etc. Train and road tracks. Toys that involve combining objects and 'putting things together'. Model toys and real world toys, home corner, etc. All types of art/craft activities. Provide guidance and visual model, demonstration, half completed, etc. gradually increase amount of choice and freedom to be creative! Role play/puppet work, etc. Initially structured and modelled, use of play scripts and play pictures moving to free choice and unsupported play
2. Social play activities (Understanding people): • Functional communication opportunities • Early conversation skills activities • Sharing opportunities • Turn-taking opportunities • Social skills games • Emotions games • Supported free play situations	Provide communicative temptations (i.e. placing items out of reach so that the individual has to request – provide a means of requesting!), sabotage! (i.e. parts of toys missing, no battery, etc.), choice boards (increasing choices) Book sharing, commenting cards and pictures Paired, group, circle and table time activities Conversation boards and scripts Shared resources and timed (using pinger, sand timer or clock) or scheduled turn-taking activities Puppet play Faces (emotions) games, how does s/he feel games, etc. Social stories and comic strips Play scripts (this is how we play—), scenarios and role play Organised and supported playground games (led by and facilitated by adult and pupils matched) Ditto classroom games Person-child interaction and intensive interaction activities

Opportunities and activities	Strategies and examples
3.Social and community based experiences • Trips to local community (e.g. shops, park, etc.) • Whole and half day trips • Short residential trips • 'Parties' and other social events • Inclusion visits to other schools (special school pupils)	Supported by photos, schedules, social stories, social scripts, lists. Increase number of participants Providing opportunity for planning trips and activities (pictorial or written mind maps, flow charts, etc.) (see problem-solving techniques below) Taking photos/video for cued recall (photo diary) after the event

ELEMENT: THINKING AND CONCEPTUAL UNDERSTANDING

Opportunities and activities	Strategies and examples
Generalisation • Across objects (conceptual understanding/semantic links, etc.) • Across people • Across environments • Across activities. Cued recall	Teach skill, practise in one situation, gradually introduce differing situations, add choice prompt and reduce prompts towards spontaneous use of skills. Use cued recall to make connections and links Cued recall: • Photos/videos • Diaries • News and communication books • Verbal recall
Generalisation from the start	Introduce multiple opportunities right from the start (e.g. teaching vocabulary using objects, pictures, photos, different style and colour – depending on pupils' level of rigidity – may need to stagger). Use skill in different areas of school/home right from the start (e.g. asking for a drink)
Reduction of prompts	Gradually reduce type, number and level of prompt (start with minimal) Start with a 'prompt' hierarchy and gradually reduce the type and level of promoting
Link skills to functional, meaningful and concrete activities and experiences (see, do and remember!)	Plan all activities within real situations/experiences and with real objects or introduce and generalise to real situations. Work with child's interests and within child's level of experience

ELEMENT: ADAPTABILITY

Note: See also the examples given within Chapter 5.

Opportunities and activities	Strategies and examples
Play-based problem-solving activities: • Puzzles • Sorting games • Construction games • Cause and effect toys	Sabotage! • Toys/games with parts missing (e.g. puzzle pieces) • Parts which don't fit (e.g. spoon too big for the pot!) • Opening boxes/lids, etc. • Make a .... use this .... • Paint and no brush, etc. • Instructions with resources missing (e.g. make a tower with blue, red and green bricks – no green). 'Find it' games What's in the box? game How do I? games What do I need? games Adult led 'staged' problems – start an activity and something goes wrong – what shall we do?

Social problem-solving activities	Partner choice making – play boards/choice spinners
	Structured play and taught play routines
	Jigs/mini-schedules
	Conversation boards
	Social stories and sentences/comic strips, etc.
	Formal social problem-solving games and activities:
	• What would happen if?
	• What should you do?
	• What should I say?
	• Problem-solving pathways
	• Comic strip conversations
	• Role play
	• Social rules games
	    ◦ How to play
	    ◦ How to ask
	Buddies and peer support

Opportunities and activities	Strategies and examples
Learning based problem solving: Problem-solving activities (of all types of activity/learning experience and at all levels)	Choice making – materials/activities (what do I need?) Sabotage! (see above) Models/lists and schedules for physical activities What do I need for…? How do I make…? Maths and science activities (concrete, practical and meaningful) Guided self-reflection (what I did, what I could have done better) White boards Diaries and note pads Make use of visually based problem-solving strategies (see below)
Personal/everyday problem-solving activities	• What do I like? • What should I wear? • How do I get to…? • What shall I play with? • What do I need for school? Support with objects, photos or symbols if needed Support with: • Choice boards • Clothing jigs and photos • Social stories • Mini-schedules and lists • Post-its
General choice making/decision-making opportunities (This area links to the development of self-knowledge)	Choices from: • Preferred vs. non-preferred items • Choice of preferred items • Choice board • Forced choice vs. free choice • Learning choices • Social choices • Personal choices • Behaviour choices (colour codes) Problem-solving pathways and decision trees

continued

Opportunities and activities	Strategies and examples
Experiencing transition and change: Small change (e.g. personal objects, classroom items, etc.) Large change (e.g. new environment, visiting, new staff) Supported change (e.g. travelling schedules and community based activities) See also Chapter 5 – Transitions	Transition and 'connecting' or using representational objects, baseboards or match backs Transition schedules Markers around building Labels (areas and objects) Marked chairs Carpet squares Position markers Social stories

D. Assessment and the monitoring of progress

This section sets out the approach to assessment and the monitoring of progress and how this links to all aspects of the flexibility curriculum and to the four Flexibility Strands. Figure 7.1 provides a visual overview of the process.

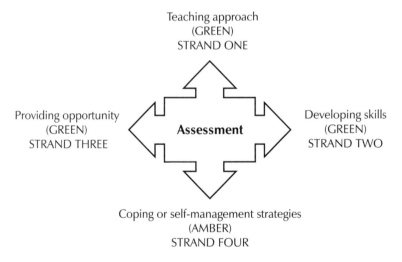

Figure 7.1: The Flexibility Strands and Assessment

This section of the policy also includes an overview of the 5P Approach Flexibility Assessment (Chapter 3) and should include examples of the materials used for assessment (the Flexibility Checklist), recording and monitoring progress (the Individual Flexibility Continuum), planning (the Flexibility Strands Planner) and target setting (the Flexibility Target Sheet).

E. Links with other policies

This section sets out links to any other relevant organisational policies such as the teaching and learning policy or behaviour policy. Any flexibility policy should also have clear links to any pupil participation or pupil voice policy.

In my experience, many schools and organisations are already addressing aspects of flexibility by making changes to the environment and approaches used, and by targeting the development of new skills. However, this is often done as part of an overall approach to intervention or as part of a behaviour intervention plan rather than identifying flexibility as a distinct and separate area.

Creating a flexibility policy and a defined flexibility curriculum highlights the importance of flexibility and places it at the centre of any approach. Since this area is linked to most aspects of learning and social development, to independence, well-being and behaviour, in my opinion this is the right place for it to be!

Chapter 8

AND FINALLY...

Adding to your GREEN Zone

This book has placed an emphasis on the importance of flexibility and its relationship with many aspects of learning and social development and of developing independence. As we have seen, having good flexibility skills is the key to independence – independence in thinking, independence in learning and independence in behaviour. Poor flexibility, whatever the underlying cause, creates significant barriers to learning and to social development and, in order to overcome those barriers, we need to support the individual to develop flexibility skills (to move along the Flexibility Continuum) and 'teachers' (whether in school, home or social situations) need to adapt their approaches while new skills emerge. This also involves providing supported opportunity for the individual to use those developing skills.

The 5P Approach to Flexibility as set out in this book provides a framework, based on the 5P Approach to behaviour intervention, which can be used at the organisational and at individual level to complement, structure and extend existing good practice. Individual elements of the 5P Approach to Flexibility can be used in assessment, intervention planning and monitoring of progress, to create safe and engaging learning environments and to develop a culture of involving the child or young person and listening to their views.

Preventing behaviour issues

We have seen that poor flexibility can so often be at the root of behaviour issues which arise. Used in conjunction with the 5P Approach to behaviour intervention, as set out in *Practical Behaviour Management Solutions for Children and Teens with Autism – The 5P Approach*, the 5P Approach to Flexibility can be used to aid both the problem-analysis and problem-solving process and the planning of intervention at GREEN and AMBER.

The 5P Approach, characterised by its distinct traffic light colours, places an emphasis on promoting and encouraging the development of skills and independence, through using the 5Ps: Profiling, Prioritising, Problem analysis, Problem solving and Planning. The 5P Approach to Flexibility materials introduced in this book also fit within this 5P framework:

- Profiling (assessment)

- Prioritising (target setting through assessment)

- Problem analysis and Problem solving (using the above)

- Planning (using the Flexibility Strands Planner).

Flexibility at the organisational and individual level

As described in the previous chapter, the 5P Approach to Flexibility and its supporting materials can be used both within the organisational level to present an overall approach to flexibility and at the individual level to create a detailed and personalised approach. Below are some brief case study examples of how the 5P Approach to Flexibility can be used in both ways.

Working at the organisational level

Here are three short examples of planning at the organisational level using the Flexibility Strands as a guide. This includes general resources, approaches and strategies which indicate the overall organisational approach. This is then tailored according to individual need.

EXAMPLE A: THE SPECIAL SCHOOL

The GREEN Zone (environment, teaching approaches, providing opportunity and developing new skills)
The school makes use of the principles of the TEACCH approach throughout the school to provide structure and guidance to the level required by each individual. All pupils have visual schedules and these are differentiated according to level of need. For example one pupil may have a written timetable, another a visual half day schedule represented by symbols, and another making use of a 'this–then' card. All pupils have access to augmentative communication such as PECS (Picture Exchange Communication System) according to their need. The school makes use of visual materials to support all transitions, with a baseboard system for supporting transition from one place to another. Teaching approaches make use of a structured and rule-based approach with clear signals for beginning and ending sessions. The school makes use

of mini-schedules to support pupils through longer learning processes. The curriculum is designed to be practical, functional and meaningful and offers opportunities for functional use of skills, choice making and problem solving.

The school targets flexibility skills within all lessons (layering). There are also specific lessons designed to teach social and play skills and problem-solving skills making use of functional activities and providing opportunities for skill generalisation. All pupils have individual flexibility targets according to identified priorities.

AMBER strategies

The staff team has access to a bank of resources used to support pupils at times when they begin to show signs of anxiety or confusion. This includes use of symbol key rings, portable choice boards, travelling schedules, etc. All staff are reminded to represent directions and to give time. Staff are reminded to represent learning activities in smaller steps with additional prompts as required. The school makes use of breaks and break areas to provide an opportunity for pupils to relax and calm.

EXAMPLE B: THE MAINSTREAM SCHOOL

The GREEN Zone

School areas are clearly labelled and areas colour coded. All students are provided with a user friendly map of the school. All students are given a school diary and weekly timetable. Teachers structure lessons clearly and signal change from plenary to individual work. All staff give reminders prior to the lesson/session end. Teachers make use of visual materials such as diagrams and flow charts to support information and students are encouraged to use mind maps, spider diagrams and writing frames to help them to structure their work. Students are provided with written instructions for homework which includes the books and resources students need in order to complete the task. LSAs (Learning Support Assistants) are used to support students within lessons where needed. These provide additional prompts and differentiation including mediated learning and supporting the think, plan and do process. This includes supporting students to identify, plan and solve problems that arise in learning or social situations.

The school provides specific sessions to teach the development of social skills and study skills (think, plan and do) which are targeted towards particular individuals who have been identified through assessment. The school has a homework club which supports those who have difficulty with planning and organising and also those who find generalising from school to home difficult ('school work is for school').

AMBER strategies

Staff are all aware of the possible signs shown by students who may become anxious or confused. They have access to a bank of resources including additional learning materials (differentiated), problem-solving pathways, etc. LSA time can be redirected to support those who appear to be struggling either academically or socially. Staff are reminded to represent directions and to give time. Staff are reminded to represent learning activities in smaller steps with additional prompts as required. The school makes use of breaks and break areas to provide an opportunity for pupils to relax and calm. Students have access to a card system to request help or a break at times of stress.

A lunchtime club room is provided for those who find lunchtime stressful. Staff supervising the club make use of visual problem-solving materials and social stories to talk through any difficult issues which might have arisen.

EXAMPLE C: THE HOME

The GREEN Zone

Toys (bedroom and house) are kept in a specific area with special toys kept in a labelled (photo) box. Clothes are similarly kept in labelled drawers. The child (and parent) have access to a communication board with key symbols (e.g. toilet, drink, garden, fruit, etc). There is a choice board next to the toy cupboard with pictures (photos) of favoured toys to aid communication. There is a clear routine for going to and arriving home from school and for bed time and meal times. Transitions to shops or visits to friends are supported by use of photos.

AMBER strategies

Parent makes use of a 'this–then–then' card for times when the child is showing signs of anxiety or confusion. Verbal information or direction is supported by sign, gesture or symbol at times when the child appears confused. Photos or transition objects are used to support difficult transitions. Parent makes use of a 'waiting bag' full of motivating toys at times when there is a need for a long wait. Parent signals the ending of a visit or activity using a finger based 5–4–3–2–1 countdown.

Working at the individual level

Here are two short examples of planning at the individual level using the 5P Approach Flexibility Assessment and the Flexibility Strands as a guide to planning.

EXAMPLE: CHILD X

Flexibility Assessment:

- Play and Social Development: Level One.
- Thinking Skills and Conceptual Understanding: Level One.
- Adaptability: Level Two.

This would place the child at an overall Level One on the Flexibility Continuum.

Flexibility Strands

1. The GREEN Zone

Work with the learning style. Create a safe, structured environment for the reduction of stress. Use a highly structured and visually supported environment (pictures or symbols), clear, and well organised with little change. Use approaches such as TEACCH. Use short visual timetables for direction. Give activities clear beginning and end. Ensure minimal change and transition. Maintain a rule based and structured approach to teaching and learning.

2. Developing flexibility skills (GREEN)

- Coping with change and transition (finishing activities and moving from place to place).
- Widening her range of interests, generalising skills between home and school.
- Developing constructive play within a small group, joint building, sharing turn taking, etc.

3. Providing opportunities to develop flexibility (GREEN)

Use planned opportunities for supported small change and transitions. Increase the choice (using choice board) of play activities. Make planned opportunity for play in different areas of the school (e.g. classroom, group room, hall, playground).

4. Teaching coping and self-management strategies (AMBER)

Ensure the prompted use of transition objects and rest stops when moving between places. Use a carpet square for group games (to denote own space and increase confidence in group situation). Provide the individual with their own box of toys and bricks to move from one area to another for play sessions.

EXAMPLE: CHILD Y

Flexibility Assessment:

- Play and Social Development: Level Four.
- Thinking Skills and Conceptual Understanding: Level Three.
- Adaptability: Level Three.

This would place the child at an overall Level Three on the Flexibility Continuum.

Flexibility Strands

1. The GREEN Zone

Teaching and developing new skills: Provide a structured approach with some challenge and change and opportunity to use newly developing skills. Encourage independent use of timetables and transition support. Increase the presentation of problem-solving opportunities, choice, change and creativity. Slowly decrease the use of prompts and increase the use of newly developing skills.

2. Developing flexibility skills (GREEN)

- Initiating and sustaining peer interaction in learning and social situations.
- Widening his range of interests and conversation.
- Developing problem-solving skills in learning (e.g. understanding the task, abstracting information from text, creating and recording response).

3. Providing opportunities to develop flexibility (GREEN)

Supported social groups and targeted social skills sessions are provided. Group and paired learning activities (supported) are used. A 'fixed' choice board for games and activities with 10 minute timer is introduced. Practical problem-solving activities and games are practised, with opportunities for increased choice and decision-making.

4. Teaching coping and self-management strategies (AMBER)

A writing frame, highlighting, mind map, colour coding, etc. is used to support written activities. Teachers/adults use a help card with student. Social stories, social strips and conversation boards aid social interaction.

Where Next?

By now you should have a good working knowledge of the 5P Approach to Flexibility and an understanding of the 5P Approach philosophy and principles. The next step is to use the ideas and materials provided with individuals and, if relevant, within your organisation and add to your own GREEN Zone!

Good luck!

INDEX